S H E P H E R D ' S   N O T E S

obeying the 10
commandmts
you'll have good credit
but not Good credit

Shepherd's Notes Titles Available

SHEPHERD'S NOTES COMMENTARY SERIES

Old Testament

0-80549-028-0	Genesis	0-80549-341-7	Psalms 101-150
0-80549-056-6	Exodus	0-80549-016-7	Proverbs
0-80549-069-8	Leviticus & Numbers	0-80549-059-0	Ecclesiastes, Song of Solomon
0-80549-027-2	Deuteronomy		
0-80549-058-2	Joshua & Judges	0-80549-197-X	Isaiah
0-80549-057-4	Ruth & Esther	0-80549-070-1	Jeremiah-Lamentations
0-80549-063-9	1 & 2 Samuel		
0-80549-007-8	1 & 2 Kings	0-80549-078-7	Ezekiel
0-80549-064-7	1 & 2 Chronicles	0-80549-015-9	Daniel
0-80549-194-5	Ezra, Nehemiah	0-80549-326-3	Hosea-Obadiah
0-80549-006-X	Job	0-80549-334-4	Jonah-Zephaniah
0-80549-339-5	Psalms 1-50	0-80549-065-5	Haggai-Malachi
0-80549-340-9	Psalms 51-100		

New Testament

1-55819-688-9	Matthew	1-55819-689-7	Philippians, Colossians, & Philemon
0-80549-071-X	Mark		
0-80549-004-3	Luke		
1-55819-693-5	John	0-80549-000-0	1 & 2 Thessalonians
1-55819-691-9	Acts	1-55819-692-7	1 & 2 Timothy, Titus
0-80549-005-1	Romans	0-80549-336-0	Hebrews
0-80549-325-5	1 Corinthians	0-80549-018-3	James
0-80549-335-2	2 Corinthians	0-80549-019-1	1 & 2 Peter & Jude
1-55819-690-0	Galatians	0-80549-214-3	1, 2 & 3 John
0-80549-327-1	Ephesians	0-80549-017-5	Revelation

SHEPHERD'S NOTES CHRISTIAN CLASSICS

0-80549-347-6	Mere Christianity-C.S.Lewis	0-80549-394-8	Miracles-C.S.Lewis
0-80549-353-0	The Problem of Pain/A Grief Observed-C.S.Lewis	0-80549-196-1	Lectures to My Students-Charles Haddon Spurgeon
0-80549-199-6	The Confessions-Augustine	0-80549-220-8	The Writings of Justin Martyr
0-80549-200-3	Calvin's Institutes	0-80549-345-X	The City of God

SHEPHERD'S NOTES-BIBLE SUMMARY SERIES

0-80549-377-8	Old Testament	0-80549-385-9	Life & Letters of Paul
0-80549-378-6	New Testament	0-80549-376-X	Manners & Customs of Bible Times
0-80549-384-0	Life & Teachings of Jesus	0-80549-380-8	Basic Christian Beliefs

SHEPHERD'S NOTES

When you need a guide through the Scriptures

Exodus

BROADMAN
&HOLMAN
PUBLISHERS

Nashville, Tennessee

© 1998
by Broadman & Holman Publishers
Nashville, Tennessee
All rights reserved
Printed in the United States of America

0–8054–9056–6
Dewey Decimal Classification: 222.12
Subject Heading: BIBLE. O.T. EXODUS
Library of Congress Card Catalog Number: 97-37021

Library of Congress Cataloging-in-Publication Data
Exodus / Robert Lintzenich, editor
        p.   cm. — (Shepherd's notes)
    ISBN 0–8054–9056–6
    1. Bible. O.T. Exodus—Study and teaching.   I. Lintzenich, Robert.
  II. Series
BS1245.5.E96   1998
222'.1207—dc21   97-37021
                                                                          CIP

6 7 8 9 10 11   10 09 08 07 06 05

Contents

FOREWORD

Dear Reader:

Shepherd's Notes are designed to give you a quick, step-by-step overview of every book of the Bible. They are not meant to be substitutes for the biblical text; rather, they are study guides intended to help you explore the wisdom of Scripture in personal or group study and to apply that wisdom successfully in your own life.

Shepherd's Notes guide you through the main themes of each book of the Bible and illuminate fascinating details through appropriate commentary and reference notes. Historical and cultural background information brings the Bible into sharper focus.

Six different icons, used throughout the series, call your attention to historical-cultural information, Old Testament and New Testament references, word pictures, unit summaries, and personal application for everyday life.

Whether you are a novice or a veteran at Bible study, I believe you will find *Shepherd's Notes* a resource that will take you to a new level in your mining and applying the riches of Scripture.

In Him,

David R. Shepherd
Editor-in-Chief

DESIGNED FOR THE BUSY USER

Shepherd's Notes for Exodus is designed to provide an easy-to-use tool for getting a quick handle on this Bible book's key features, and for gaining an understanding of its message. Information available in more difficult-to-use reference works has been incorporated into the *Shepherd's Notes* format. This brings you the benefits of many advanced and expensive works packed into one small volume.

Shepherd's Notes are for laymen, pastors, teachers, small group leaders, and participants, as well as the classroom student. Enrich your personal study or quiet time. Shorten your class or small-group preparation time as you gain valuable insights into the truths of God's Word that you can pass along to your students or group members.

DESIGNED FOR QUICK ACCESS

Bible students with time constraints will especially appreciate the time-saving features built into *Shepherd's Notes*. All features are intended to aid a quick and concise encounter with the heart of the message.

Concise Commentary. The narrative of Exodus is replete with characters, places, and events. Short sections provide quick "snapshots" of the running narrative, highlighting important points.

Outlined Text. A comprehensive outline covers the entire text of Exodus. This is a valuable feature for following the narrative's flow, allowing for a quick, easy way to locate a particular passage.

Shepherd's Notes. These summary statements appear at the close of every key section of the narrative. While functioning in part as a quick summary, they also deliver the essence of the message presented in the sections which they cover.

Icons. Various icons in the margin highlight recurring themes in Exodus, aiding in selective searching or tracing of those themes.

Sidebars and Charts. These specially selected features provide additional background information to your study or preparation. Charts offer a quick overview of important subjects. Sidebars include definitions as well as cultural, historical, and biblical information.

Questions to Guide Your Study. These thought-provoking questions and discussion starters are designed to encourage interaction with the truth and principles of God's Word.

DESIGNED TO WORK FOR YOU

Personal study. Using the *Shepherd's Notes* with a passage of Scripture can enlighten your study and take it to a new level. At your fingertips is information that would require searching several volumes to find. In addition, many points of application occur throughout the volume, contributing to personal growth.

Teaching. Outlines frame the text of Exodus, providing a logical presentation of the message. Capsule thoughts designated as "Shepherd's Notes" provide summary statements for presenting the essence of key points and events. Application icons point out personal application of the message of Exodus, and Historical Context icons indicate where cultural and historical background information is supplied.

Group Study. *Shepherd's Notes* can be an excellent companion volume to use for gaining a quick but accurate understanding of the message of a Bible book. Each group member can benefit by having his or her own copy. The *Notes* format accommodates the study of or the tracing of themes throughout Exodus. Leaders may use its flexible features to prepare for group sessions or use them during group sessions. The questions to guide your study can spark discussion of the key points and truths of the message of Exodus.

LIST OF MARGIN ICONS USED IN LUKE

 Shepherd's Notes. Placed at the end of each section, a capsule statement that provides the reader with the essence of the message of that section.

 Old Testament Reference. Used when the writer refers to Old Testament Scripture passages that are related or have a bearing on the passage's understanding or interpretation.

 New Testament Reference. Used when the writer refers to New Testament passages that are related to or have a bearing on the passage's understanding or interpretation.

 Historical Background. To indicate historical, cultural, geographical, or biographical information that sheds light on the understanding or interpretation of a passage.

 Personal Application. Used when the text provides a personal or universal application of truth.

 Word Picture. Indicates that the meaning of a specific word or phrase is illustrated so as to shed light on it.

The Book of Exodus is the story of two covenant partners—God and Israel. Exodus narrates how Israel became the people of God and sets forth the covenant terms by which the nation was expected to live as God's people.

The most important event in the Old Testament historically and theologically is Israel's deliverance from slavery in Egypt. Yet the liberation from Egypt is incomplete without the covenant at Mount Sinai.

Exodus can be considered the central book of the Old Testament since it reports God's basic saving act for Israel in the Exodus from Egypt and His making of His covenant with the nation destined to be His kingdom of priests.

AUTHOR

There is no statement in the book itself or in the rest of the Bible that Moses wrote the Book of Exodus. Nevertheless, the Old and New Testaments reflect the view that the Pentateuch was a unified work of a single author, Moses (Josh. 1:7–8; 8:31; 23:6; 1 Kings 2:3; 2 Kings 14:6; 2 Chron. 34:14; Neh. 8:1; 13:1; Luke 20:28; John 1:45; Acts 3:22).

AUDIENCE

After forty years of wilderness wandering, the Israelites were about to cross the Jordan River and begin the conquest and settlement of Canaan. The old, rebellious generation had died. The new generation had to hear and respond to the covenant that God had made with their parents at Sinai. Moses must inform God's people of their identity and focus.

PURPOSE

The story of the Exodus would educate the people of Israel about their identity, their history, their role among the nations, and their future. The sovereign God of all nations had overthrown Egypt and redeemed Israel. God was offering to this one nation a covenant that would allow them the privilege of serving all peoples as "a kingdom of priests and a holy nation."

STRUCTURE AND CONTENT

The story of Exodus consists of six magnificent scenes, each of them revealing something about Israel's God. The six scenes, however, can be grouped into three main episodes. First, the people are brought from Egypt to Mount Sinai. Second, they are presented with the covenant laws and instructions. Finally, the covenant relationship between God and people is established, broken, restored, and renewed.

6 SCENES

THEOLOGY

The theology of Exodus is rooted in redemption and servanthood. It centers in the truth that a chosen people were delivered from bondage to a hostile power by the mighty works of the Lord. Yet their redemption brought them to a point of decision. What would they do with God's offer to make them the servant people that had been promised long ago to Abraham? Their willing acceptance of this generous offer then obligated them to its conditions—conditions that were spelled out in the Ten Commandments and the Book of the Covenant.

Exodus defines the character of the covenant partners: God and Israel. God's character is revealed both through His name and His acts. Israel's character is defined by the people's reaction to the Sinai covenant. If it were accepted and lived out, the covenant would result in Israel's being God's "treasured possession," a chosen "kingdom of priests," and a "holy nation."

BOOK	THEMATIC FOCUS
Genesis 1–11	Beginnings
Genesis 12–50	Promise
Exodus	Redemption
Leviticus	Holiness
Numbers	Testing
Deuteronomy	Instruction

The grand theme of the Pentateuch is restoration. God chooses to restore His people to a position in which they can have a relationship with Him. The thematic focus of Exodus is redemption. God redeems Israel from slavery and offers them a covenant relationship in which they will become a channel of reconciliation to an alienated world.

The meaning of Exodus must be understood within its position in the Pentateuch, the first five books of the Old Testament.

THE MEANING OF EXODUS FOR TODAY

The Exodus deliverance is to the Old Testament what the death and resurrection of Christ are to the New Testament: the central, definitive act in which God intervenes to save His people. Just as the proclamation of God's saving acts in the Exodus is prominent in Israel's worship (Ps. 136:10–16), so Christian worship focuses on God's saving act in Christ.

central.
definitive
Act

The Exodus deliverance, the Sinai covenant, and the wilderness journey all provide models of the Christian life. The believer, having already and unconditionally been adopted into the family of God, undertakes his or her own

3

"exodus" from bondage to sin and evil. God's saving act in Christ is the basis for the Christian's hope of future salvation (Rom. 8:28–39).

The Exodus story illustrates how God's acts of redemption call for a response from God's people. Each individual today must make a choice at a personal "Mount Sinai," a choice to accept or reject servanthood under a new covenant. God's saving act in Christ is the basis for the call to live a Christlike life.

> "For when I brought your forefathers out of Egypt and spoke to them, I did not just give them commands about burnt offerings and sacrifices, but I gave them this command: Obey me, and I will be your God and you will be my people" (Jer. 7:22–23).

When the Israelites accepted the Sinai covenant, they were still in the wilderness, far from the Promised Land. Acceptance for believers means living out their kingdom pilgrimage in the wilderness of this world system. Yet they are not alone on the pilgrimage, for God guides, protects, and abides within them as they press toward and anticipate the eternal Land of Promise to come.

In the meeting with Israel at Mount Sinai, God demanded that the people live under the conditions of the covenant. He demands that same adherence to His unchanging standards of all who call themselves His people. The statutes designed specifically for Old Testament Israel exemplify standards of holiness and integrity that are part and parcel of God's expectations for His people throughout history.

The first section of the Book of Exodus, 1:1–13:16, focuses on the saving presence of God. That presence would eventually result in the liberation of Israel from Egyptian slavery.

GOD'S PRESENCE WITH HIS OPPRESSED PEOPLE (1:1–22)

The Book of Genesis ends with Joseph taking his father's family into Egypt to avoid the harsh sufferings of famine. The Book of Exodus takes up the story of the children of Jacob in Egypt. God had preserved Israel from famine when He sent Joseph to Egypt. Now God preserves His people through the oppression of slavery.

God Prospers His Oppressed People (1:1–7)

The Exodus story begins by recalling the descent of Jacob and his sons to Egypt, first recounted in Gen. 46. The link to Genesis reminds us that God sent Israel into Egypt to deliver them from famine. Now, their prosperity and success in their new land (Exod. 1:7) shows that Israel is still receiving God's blessing, as promised to Abraham, "I will make you into a great nation" (Gen. 12:2).

Oppressed by Forced Labor and Extermination (1:8–22)

Egyptian hospitality did not long outlive Joseph. When Joseph, second in command to Pharaoh, had delivered Egypt from famine, the Israelites were welcomed in the land. But in the Book of Exodus, Egypt was now under a new pharaoh "who did not know about Joseph" (1:8), and the Israelites were feared as foreigners. Egypt's welcome turned to bitter hostility and oppression.

The Hyksos Pharaohs

The Hyksos were not native Egyptians. Later Egyptians tried to erase all evidence of the period when the Hyksos ruled Egypt. Joseph was related ethnically to the Semitic Hyksos rulers, and it is likely that he served a Hyksos pharaoh. The later Egyptian pharaoh who "did not know about Joseph" (1:8) did not "know" about him in a political or historical sense. Neither would an Egyptian pharaoh have considered Joseph to be significant, since native Egyptians regarded Semites with contempt.

Fear of the prospering Hebrews led the pharaoh to take drastic actions. Plan A was to put the Hebrew people under forced labor (1:11–14). As slave laborers, the Hebrews built the store cities of Pithom and Rameses. Surprisingly, Plan A failed; despite the exhaustion from their work, Egypt's slaves continued to multiply.

When Plan A did not work, Pharaoh devised a more devious Plan B. He would prevent the Hebrews' growth by exterminating their male newborns (1:15–19). Yet this plan, too, was confounded by the civil disobedience of the Hebrew midwives Shiphrah and Puah. In frustration, Pharaoh ordered his people to destroy all male Hebrew babies.

Midwives Who Feared God?

Shiphrah and Puah are the two Hebrew midwives who disobeyed Pharaoh's orders to kill male Hebrew infants (1:15). Why did they resist Pharaoh, risking their own lives? Certainly they had compassion for their own Hebrew people, and thus would have not wanted to carry out Pharaoh's command. But their ultimate motive was because they "feared God" (1:17). They valued God's gift of human life more highly than obedience to Pharaoh. For their faithfulness God rewarded them with families of their own (1:21).

■ *What is significant about this part of Israel's*
■ *history is that God, not Egypt's new king,*
■ *was in control. Even during years of oppres-*
■ *sion God was with Israel and caused them to*
■ *prosper (1:12, 20).*

QUESTIONS TO GUIDE YOUR STUDY

1. What policies did the Egyptian pharaoh adopt in order to keep the Hebrews from becoming too numerous?
2. How was God involved in preserving the lives of His oppressed people?
3. How should we respond when, like the Hebrew midwives, we are asked to do something that is against God's purposes for humankind?

Rescued by Pharaoh's daughter, Moses was reared by his mother, who introduced him to the God of Israel.

GOD PROTECTS THE YOUNG MOSES (2:1–22)

Moses would become the human agent to bring about God's deliverance of Israel. What is evident about the early life of Moses is God's saving presence. God delivered the baby Moses from danger, and the child grew up in Pharaoh's court as the son of Pharaoh's own daughter.

The Birth of Moses (2:1–10)

When his Levite parents could no longer hide the growing baby, Moses' mother constructed an ark, a basket of bulrushes made waterproof with bitumen and pitch, and placed it in the Nile River. How alarmed Moses' sister must have been to witness an apparent twist of fate when it was Pharaoh's own daughter who came to the river, found the ark, and recognized the child as a Hebrew!

But God was active in the infant's life. Rather than killing him as her father had commanded, the Egyptian princess showed compassion. Not only was the baby rescued from the Nile, but at the initiation of his sister, he was committed to the care of a wet nurse. Of course, under the hand and plan of God, the wet nurse turned out to be the baby's own mother (2:8–9).

The baby grew as a child, and his mother delivered him to the princess. As a part of the adoption procedure, the princess named the child Moses.

bAsket Like An ARk

soN Egyptian

The Name "Moses"

In Egyptian, the name *Moses* meant "son," appearing in the names of such pharaohs as Ah*mose* and Thut*mose*. The daughter of Pharaoh would have named Moses when she adopted him into her royal family. She chose the personal name *Moses* which sounds like the Hebrew word for "draw out." Thus "Moses" also has spiritual significance as the name of the baby "drawn out of the water."

dRAw out HEbReu

7

During his first forty years in the courts of the pharaoh's daughter, Moses undoubtedly learned many administrative, literary, and legal skills that would serve him well as Israel's leader and lawgiver. During the next forty years in the Midianite wilderness, Moses learned practical skills that would help him in leading Israel through the wilderness.

The Name "Gershom"

The personal name *Gershom* means "sojourner there" or "expelled one." In Exodus, the name is interpreted to mean "stranger" or "alien," since the Hebrew word *ger* means "sojourner." This son of Moses was born in Midian. Although Moses was settled in Midian, he knew he was a only a "sojourner" there. Moses belonged with his people, and they were far from him in Egypt.

■ *The first months of Moses' life were certainly*
■ *not normal. Some observers of the events sur-*
■ *rounding Moses' birth and deliverance would*
■ *see only coincidence. But those observing by*
■ *faith see the work of God, who uses life's nor-*
■ *mal affairs to accomplish a greater purpose.*

Moses Exiled to Midian (2:11–22)

The young Moses grew to maturity in the palace of the king who had sought to kill him. Although he surely enjoyed the privileges of the Egyptian royal court, Moses never forgot his Israelite heritage. When he saw a fellow Hebrew being abused, he knew that this was "one of his own people" (2:11). Killing the offending Egyptian was possibly a heroic act, but it was also rash. In the wake of this violent deed, Moses was forced to flee to Midian, away from his people.

Moses' Life in Midian (2:15–22)

It appears that Moses was able to build a new life for himself in Midian. Again he intervened in the face of oppression, rescuing seven female shepherds, whose father was a priest of Midian. Moses was invited to live and work under the protection of the priest's hospitality. Eventually one of the Midianite's daughters became Moses' wife.

Moses' new life was one of idyllic peace, taking care of the priest's sheep and fathering a child by his wife Zipporah. But all was not well, for Moses was at a distance from his own people. He named his first son "Gershom," which in Hebrew refers to a sojourner. Moses was only sojourning in Midian because his people in Egypt needed him.

- *Moses' life was providentially spared as an*
- *infant, for God had a plan for him. God was*
- *also preparing Moses to carry out the*
- *divine plan.*

God Remembers His Covenant (2:23–25)

While Moses was in Midian, some things were changing in Egypt. The pharaoh from whom Moses fled died. Other things were not changing: A new pharaoh did not bring new conditions for the Hebrews, who remained oppressed. What also had not changed was God's covenant with Abraham to make his descendants a great nation. God was concerned about the plight of His people in Egypt (2:25).

- *The pharaohs come and go (1:8; 2:23), but*
- *the Lord of history remains the same and*
- *stands forever.*

QUESTIONS TO GUIDE YOUR STUDY

1. How did God use the love and compassion of a Hebrew mother and an Egyptian princess to defeat Pharaoh's plan?
2. Moses hid the dead Egyptian in the sand (2:12). Is it possible for us to hide our sins and pretend they never happened?
3. How did Moses' rash act of killing the Egyptian interrupt God's greater purpose?

Exodus reveals the character of God through His name. The most important of God's names is the covenant name *Yahweh*, translated "the LORD."

GOD REVEALS HIS PRESENCE (3:1–4:17)

The death of the former king of Egypt paved the way for Moses to return to Egypt. But first the eternal God had to reveal Himself to Moses. God did this at Mount Horeb (Sinai) in a convincing display of His power and purposes.

Revelation in the Burning Bush (3:1–6)

Horeb is an alternative name for Mount Sinai, the place where Moses witnessed a burning bush that was not consumed. The bush, which attracted Moses' attention, was only one part of this marvelous appearance of the Lord to Moses. Several other features of the experience convinced Moses that he was in the presence of the living God.

The angel of the LORD. This angel was a messenger of God who cannot be distinguished from God Himself. The angel appeared to Moses, but it was God who spoke (3:2, 4).

Flames of fire. Fire often symbolizes holiness and equates God's presence with His holiness. The fire of the bush indicated the holy power of a God, who is unsearchable, incomprehensible, incomparable, great, wonderful, and exalted.

Holy ground. The place where Moses stood had been set apart for God and was called "holy" because God was present. Moses was warned

God of Your Fathers

The phrase "God of the fathers" designates the God of the patriarchs. Sometimes the name of a particular patriarch is given: "The God of Abraham" or "the God of Isaac" (Exod. 3:6). Each of the patriarchs apparently had a special name for God, resulting in names like "Fear of Isaac" (Gen. 31:42) and "Mighty One of Jacob" (Gen. 49:24).

The burning bush incident emphasized the continuity between the God who guided the patriarchs and the God who revealed Himself to Moses. Moses' generation was linked to the earlier patriarchal generations, and especially to the promises God made to the patriarchs. The God of their fathers would bless them just as He had promised their fathers (Deut. 1:11).

not to come closer, for the place was filled with superhuman and potentially fatal power.

God of Abraham. The Lord identified Himself as the God of the ancestors of Israel—Abraham, Isaac, Jacob. Yet He also described Himself to Moses as the "God of your father"(3:6). This was the God whom Moses' parents had worshiped and the God Moses likely heard of as his mother nursed him during his early years.

This encounter completely overwhelmed Moses, and he was afraid to look at God. Such a personal experience of God's holy presence evoked veneration or awe, being frightening beyond belief.

God's holiness should remind us of our lowly status as creatures before the mighty God who created us and holds us in His hand.

■ *Because Moses was receptive to God appear-*
■ *ing in an unexpected place, God was able to*
■ *speak to him.*

Who Is This God? (3:7–22)

The event at the burning bush introduced Moses to the critical character of the heroic work to which God was calling him. God was aware of His people's suffering and was coming now to fulfill His pledge of deliverance and a home land. Now, at Horeb, God was calling Moses to lead Israel out of Egypt. Moses' response is summarized by two questions: Who am I? Who are You?

Who am I? The first question could be rephrased: Am I qualified to be this leader? Moses felt inadequate for the task. Yet what was crucial was not Moses' "Who am I?" but God's "I

"I AM"

God revealed His name *Yahweh* in the context of redemption of Israel from slavery. The Hebrew name means "I am," and in response to Moses' request for a name, God answered by identifying Himself as the living God: "I am who I am" (3:14). The Hebrew phrase can also be translated as "I cause to be what is," identifying God as the one who acts in creation and redemptive history. The Lord's name is the concrete confirmation that God who "is" will "make things happen" and fulfill His promises.

11

will be with you" (3:11–12). God promised Moses that he would successfully lead the people from Egypt back to the mountain where he was now standing.

Who are you? Moses knew of the God of his fathers and of the ancient covenant promises, but he needed to know precisely how his God would identify Himself to His people. People in the ancient world placed much significance on the meaning of a person's name. For them, a name expressed essence. To know the name of a person was to know that person's total character and nature.

■ *God offered Moses a distinctive name—I*
■ *AM—as the essential key for Moses' author-*
■ *ity. This strange formula played on God's*
■ *promise to Moses to be present with him in*
■ *his special commission.*

QUESTIONS TO GUIDE YOUR STUDY

1. Would Moses have thought it safe for him to return to Egypt? How much did he risk to follow God's command to lead the people from Egypt?
2. What did God reveal to Moses about His true nature?
3. How did God assure Moses that he could successfully fulfill the task that He had assigned him?

Moses was a reluctant leader. He questioned his own abilities; he questioned whether the people would respond; he made excuses and even begged God to find someone else. But ultimately Moses did obey and prepared to confront the pharaoh of Egypt.

Like Moses, we often conjure up excuses by emphasizing our weaknesses (4:10). In response, God offers solutions that emphasize His power and strengths (4:11–12).

SIGNS OF GOD'S PRESENCE (4:1–17)

Moses doubted that the people would accept his leadership or believe his report about the burning bush experience. So God gave Moses some tangible evidence of His presence.

Divine Power at Work (4:2–9)

God gave Moses three signs that he could perform before the people and before Pharaoh. Each of the first two signs was obviously the work of God, as He turned Moses' shepherd's staff into a snake and caused Moses' hand to become leprous. Should more evidence be needed, God would turn water from the Nile River into blood.

Failing to Believe (4:10–17)

Still not confident of success, Moses argued that he was not articulate. To quieten Moses' objections once more, God promised to make his brother Aaron his spokesman.

- We can never escape feelings of inadequacy,
- fears of how others will react, or anxiety over
- problems and difficulties that might arise.
- What we can do is to trust in God's power to
- help us accomplish His purposes.

Bridegroom of Blood

Circumcision was a sign of the covenant between God and the patriarch Abraham (Gen. 17:10). For Israel, it became an external sign of an internal singularity of devotion to the Lord. Moses apparently disobeyed God by not circumcising his son; and Zipporah, though she seems not to have approved of the ritual, recognized its necessity.

The Journey to Egypt Begins (4:18–26)

Moses at last yielded to God and started for Egypt, bearing God's message for Pharaoh. Along the way, in an alarming encounter, God met Moses and threatened to kill him. The explanation for this strange episode may lie in Zipporah's quick intervention: by circumcising their son Gershom, she saved Moses' life. Moses had agreed to lead the circumcised people of Israel, but he had failed to circumcise his own son. Zipporah hastily circumcised her son in obedience to God's covenant requirements.

Aaron—Spokesman and Brother (4:27–31)

At the edge of the desert Moses met his brother Aaron and together they entered Egypt. After Aaron related to the elders of Israel all that God had spoken to Moses, the elders and the people responded with faith, bowing themselves before the Lord.

■ *In spite of Moses' slowness in responding to*
■ *the call of the Lord on Mount Horeb, he went*
■ *on in faith to challenge the political and mil-*
■ *itary structures of one of the most powerful*
■ *nations on earth.*

QUESTIONS TO GUIDE YOUR STUDY

1. What valid excuses can we offer to God in order to convince Him that what He asks of us cannot really be accomplished?

2. In how many different ways did God empower Moses for the task He was asking him to do?

3. Moses could not represent God to the people while he himself failed to follow God's requirements of circumcision. Can

you effectively tell others about your faith if you disobey God's commandments for holy living?

EXODUS 5 · · · · · · · · · · · · · · · · · ·

God knew the situation of His people. Their deliverance was already in progress, as the saving God had called out a leader to communicate His will and to face their enemies.

GOD'S LEADER DELIVERS GOD'S MESSAGE (5:1–21)

Moses returned to Egypt to negotiate with Pharaoh for the freedom of the Israelite people. The negotiation narratives of Exodus 5–12 depict Moses, the hero, in one scene of failure after another.

Pharaoh Rejects the Lord (5:1–14)

Pharaoh's question, "Who is the LORD, that I should obey him and let Israel go?" (5:2), sets the stage for the conflict that dominates the scene through Exodus 15.

At first Moses delivered God's message in a straightforward manner: "Let My people go" (5:1). He introduced God to Pharaoh as "the God of Israel." Neither the message nor the approach impressed Egypt's king. To accept the Hebrew slaves as the "nation Israel" and to honor their God's wishes was more than Pharaoh was willing to consider.

Moses tried a different approach, referring to the "God of the Hebrews" (5:3), meaning the God of Pharaoh's Hebrew slaves. This second attempt was no more successful, and now Pharaoh reacted by ordering more work for the slaves.

Pharaoh

The title *Pharaoh* means "great house." Egyptians applied the title to their kings from about 1500 B.C. on. An ancient pharaoh was an absolute monarch and considered to be a god himself. An example of his divine power was his daily performing of an early morning ritual in which he broke the seal to the statue of the sun god, waking the deity up with a prayer.

■ *Pharaoh could not understand the spiritual*
■ *significance of Moses' request. He had no*
■ *experience with Israel's God and saw no need*
■ *for the people to worship Him. Reacting like*
■ *an earthly minded person, Pharaoh ordered,*
■ *"Gather your own straw and keep making*
■ *those bricks!"*

The People Reject Moses (5:15–21)

Pharaoh had made life harder for the Israelites, and their leaders—the foremen—went to Pharaoh to correct the situation. At first they blamed Pharaoh's "own people" (5:16)—the slave drivers. Receiving no relief from Pharaoh, they griped to Moses and Aaron, blaming them for the current poor relations between them and the Egyptians.

■ *Israel's leaders found it easy to believe in*
■ *God when signs were being performed before*
■ *their eyes (4:29–31). When problems arose,*
■ *though, they looked for someone to*
■ *blame—the slave drivers or Moses and*
■ *Aaron. Worse, they began to lose faith that*
■ *God was going to deliver them from Egyp-*
■ *tian slavery.*

QUESTIONS TO GUIDE YOUR STUDY

1. We are excited about our faith and our experience with God, but others do not know our God and are not interested. Should we continue to speak about spiritual things?

2. What should be our reaction when obeying God becomes a struggle or makes our life harder?

3. When things go wrong, will blaming our leaders make our situation better?

EXODUS 6

The people were disappointed that Moses and Aaron had not helped them. Moses was disappointed that God had not delivered the people. Pharaoh had not reacted the way Moses had thought he would. It was time to regroup.

GOD PROMISES DELIVERANCE TO A DEAF PEOPLE (5:22–6:12)

A stubborn Pharaoh had intensified the Israelites' sufferings, and now Moses had to face a discouraged and disgruntled people. Bitter, Moses accused God. Nevertheless, God's message to Moses and to the people did not change.

Renewing the Divine Call (5:22–6:8)

God renewed His pledge to be with Israel in deliverance—a pledge grounded securely in His covenant name. God had not forgotten that covenant, and He now commanded Moses to go back to Pharaoh with another message.

Faltering Confidence (6:9–12)

When Moses reported to the Israelites, as God instructed him, the people did not believe. The first time Moses came to them, they had accepted the message readily. But their earlier discouragements had left them extremely hesitant to think that their situation would change this time.

God Almighty

One Hebrew name for God is *El Shaddai*, meaning "God Almighty" (6:3). It was particularly by this name that God was known to Abraham and the patriarchs (Gen. 17:1), but God Almighty was to some extent replaced by the name which God revealed to Moses: Yahweh, translated "the Lord."

Genealogy

A genealogy is a family record often listing several people of a particular generation. The children of each son and the children of the next generation are listed, usually for a particular purpose. By providing the relationships between various groups, the genealogy shows a person's right to hold an office or function. For example, the genealogy of Exod. 6:13–25, which named certain sons of Jacob, showed Moses' and Aaron's right to lead Israel out of Egypt.

■ *Moses was impatient that God did not imme-*
■ *diately rescue the people. Indeed, things had*
■ *even become worse! When God renewed His*
■ *promise of deliverance, the people did not*
■ *believe. When the people disbelieved, Moses*
■ *lost confidence that he, with his limited*
■ *speaking abilities, could get Pharaoh to*
■ *believe. Everyone was underestimating*
■ *God's power.*

REAFFIRMING THE MISSION (6:13–7:7)

Difficulties, problems, and hard times can be very disruptive to any human endeavor. Pharaoh's response had certainly disrupted Moses' mission. The people were doubting Moses as a leader, and Moses himself was again focusing on his personal weaknesses—his "faltering lips" (6:12). At this point, the Book of Exodus reaffirms the mission.

The Genealogy of Moses and Aaron (6:13–27)

The crisis of faith in Moses' and Aaron's leadership demanded reassurance that they were the ones to lead Israel. The genealogy of Exod. 6:14–25 offered that reassurance and established their credentials.

■ *Reuben, Simeon, and Levi, as the older sons*
■ *of Jacob, had led the Israelites into Egypt.*
■ *Aaron and Moses, descendants of Levi,*
■ *would now lead Israel out. God was working*
■ *through the family line!*

Pharaoh did not know the Lord, but God would not let him remain ignorant. The Egyptian king would be confronted by Moses, who represented the Lord Himself.

Reaffirming Insecure Leaders (6:28–7:7)

Moses saw himself as inferior to Pharaoh, convinced that the Egyptian king would never listen to him. God saw things differently. Through God's divine power, Moses would actually seem like God Himself to Pharaoh. God would give Moses authority over Pharaoh.

QUESTIONS TO GUIDE YOUR STUDY

1. Why were the people unwilling to believe the promises that they would be delivered?
2. How is God's plan for our lives often a bigger picture than the details of our day-to-day experiences?
3. What can we learn about living the Christian life by observing the lives and examples of our ancestors?

CONFRONTATIONS WITHOUT COMPROMISE (7:8–11:10)

Again and again Moses and Aaron would confront Pharaoh, demanding that he let their people leave Egypt. In spite of the many signs, wonders, and plagues revealing the presence of the Lord, the king of Egypt would not relent. There seemed to be no compromise possible between these negotiators.

The First Sign (7:8–13)

At the burning bush encounter, God provided Moses with three signs of God's presence and

Hardness of Heart

One way of resisting God is for a person to "harden his heart." Pharaoh hardened his heart as he refused to let the Israelites go. A puzzling aspect of the contest between God and Pharaoh is the statement that *God* hardened Pharaoh's heart. God's hardening seems to be a punishment which comes as the consequence of Pharaoh's own initial self hardening. The Egyptian king hardened his own heart and then became confirmed in his stubbornness.

First Cycle of Plagues

PLAGUE	INITIATION	RESULT	SCRIPTURE
One: Water to blood	Moses confronts Pharaoh in the morning	Waters of the Nile turn to blood	Exod. 7:14–24
Two: Frogs	Moses goes to Pharaoh	Frogs infest the land of Egypt	Exod. 7:25—8:15
Three: Gnats	Plague is unannounced	Small stinging insects infest the land of Egypt	Exod. 8:16–19

power (4:1–9). The Israelite people witnessed the signs and believed (4:30–31). Now before Pharaoh, Aaron's staff became a snake and swallowed the staffs of the Egyptian magicians. Even though God demonstrated His power to be greater than that of Egypt's gods, Pharaoh was unimpressed and still refused to let the people go.

The Plagues Begin and the Nile River Becomes Blood (7:14–24)

The confrontations between Pharaoh and Moses are interesting for their changing dynamics. On one hand, there is the continuing contest of deities—Moses' God versus the gods of Egypt. The Lord increasingly demonstrated His superiority. On another hand, there is the changing reactions of pharaoh and the Egyptians. At first they were unconcerned, but gradually they began to recognize the power of God.

Round one of the conflict included three plagues: blood, frogs, gnats. In the first plague waters of the River Nile were turned into blood.

The Nile was the major river considered the "life" of ancient Egypt. As an agricultural community, Egypt was unique in not being dependent on rainfall. Egypt's secret was the black silt deposited on its fields by the annual flooding of the Nile. This silt was remarkably fertile. Turning the Nile to blood was an attack on the basis of Egypt's wealth. Nevertheless, Egypt's magicians duplicated the feat, and Pharaoh was not impressed.

- Egypt's magicians could duplicate some of
- God's signs, possibly by magical tricks or
- illusions. What they could not do was to
- eliminate God's work and return Egypt to
- normal. Whatever the nature of the magi-
- cians' power, it was not a match for God.

QUESTIONS TO GUIDE YOUR STUDY

1. Why should we base our faith more on God's promises than on physical signs of His presence?
2. Would miracles and supernatural events make it easier to believe in God? Does God perform some "miracles" that are not supernatural?

Jannes and Jambres

Although the names do not appear in the Old Testament, Rabbinic tradition identified Jannes and Jambres as being among those Egyptian magicians who sought to duplicate for Pharaoh the miracles performed by Moses (7:22). Their names appear in a Qumran scroll, and they are mentioned by Eusebius of Caesarea and by Paul in his letter to Timothy (2 Tim. 3:8).

EXODUS 8

God worked in the forces of nature to show His unequalled power. The Egyptians had gods to protect them from certain problems caused by nature. Moses' God, however, revealed His superior power by inflicting Egypt with the plagues on His own schedule.

Plague Two: Frogs (7:25–8:15)

In the second plague, the land was filled with frogs. Again the Egyptian magicians were able to duplicate the feat. Pharaoh, however, did begin to recognize the Lord's might, requesting that Moses and Aaron pray "to the Lord" to remove the frogs (8:8).

Signs and Wonders

Signs and wonders are words used to describe the miraculous. They describe God's supernatural activity—a special manifestation of His power (8:23). Pharaoh is proof that miraculous signs will not compel people to believe in God. It is by faith, not persuasion, that we praise the Lord as He "who alone does marvelous deeds" (Ps. 72:18).

■ *The frogs plagued the palace as well as the*
■ *mud-brick structures in which many Egyp-*
■ *tians lived. Wealth and power will not pro-*
■ *tect a person from God's judgments.*

Plague Three: Gnats (8:16–19)

In the third plague, the dust throughout Egypt became gnats. Significantly, the magicians for the first time were unable to duplicate Moses' and Aaron's wonder. This final plague of round one exceeded the magical powers of their secret arts, and they thus acknowledged God's power, saying; "This is the finger of God" (8:19). Refusing to heed his own magicians, Pharaoh's heart remained hard.

Second Cycle of Plagues

PLAGUE	INITIATION	RESULT	SCRIPTURE
Four: Flies	Moses confronts Pharaoh in the morning	Swarms of flies infest the land of Egypt	Exod. 8:20–32
Five: Disease on livestock	Moses goes to Pharaoh	Disease infests the cattle belonging to Egyptians	Exod. 9:1–7
Six: Boils	Plague is unannounced	A skin disease infects the Egyptians	Exod. 9:8–12

Plague Four: Flies (8:20–32)

Round two of the conflict consisted of another three plagues: flies, livestock disease, and boils. The plague of flies demonstrated that the Lord was present in Egypt. God showed that He controlled where this fourth plague would strike; the flies swarmed everywhere in Egypt except the land of Goshen, where the Hebrews lived.

Pharaoh now realized that he would have to deal with Moses' God, so he tried a compromise. He would allow the Hebrews to worship the Lord if they remained in Egypt (8:25). For Moses to obey the Lord required him to reject Pharaoh's offer. The people must leave Egypt. Offering another compromise, Pharaoh said the Hebrews could go, as long as they did not go far (8:28). Egypt's king was beginning to bend, but when the flies were gone he again hardened his heart.

■ *Pharaoh seemed to be saying that he would*
■ *let the people go, but he kept adding condi-*
■ *tions. Either they must not leave Egypt, or if*
■ *they did they must not go far into the desert.*
■ *Political deceit cannot defeat God's purposes.*

QUESTIONS TO GUIDE YOUR STUDY

1. In what ways can our refusal to obey God affect the lives of other people?
2. People will sometimes oppose or ridicule our efforts to do God's will. Should we look for a compromise action that will accomplish most of what God wants, while being more pleasing to others?
3. Pharaoh's heart remained hardened even after his magicians had recognized the power of God. How can we avoid becoming so set in our positions that we are blind to the truth that others see?

The previous plagues had caused great discomfort, afflicting both humans and animals. The next plagues, however, would begin to destroy the Egyptians' property.

Plague Five: Livestock Disease (9:1–7)

The fifth plague inflicted a grievous disease on livestock in the fields. The Lord revealed His presence by setting the time that the disease would strike. Pharaoh was to expect it the next day (9:5).

The uniqueness of this plague was evident in its intensity. The report that "*all* the livestock of the Egyptians died" (9:6, author's emphasis) is a figure of speech, used to indicate the severity of this "terrible plague" (9:3). In actuality, some Egyptian livestock survived only to be struck by the next plagues (9:10, 20–21).

Again God distinguished between the Egyptians and His own people; none of the livestock belonging to the Israelites were affected. Pharaoh took another step toward recognizing the Lord's presence when he investigated to see whether the Israelite animals really were unaffected, as Moses and Aaron had announced. Yet even this sign did not motivate Pharaoh to let the people go.

Paul and the Plagues

The apostle Paul referred to the plagues to emphasize the sovereignty of God. Even Pharaoh's hardening of his own heart was part of God's purpose. Through the events of the plagues, Israel and Egypt would come to know the Lord and His power, and that is why God raised Pharaoh up (Rom. 9:17).

■ *Pharaoh's investigation showed that he was*
■ *at least curious as to whether the Israelites*
■ *had been protected by their God. Curiosity*
■ *about God is not sufficient to establish a rela-*
■ *tionship with Him. God seeks true repen-*
■ *tance and faith.*

Plague Six: Boils (9:8–12)

The last plague of this round touched the Egyptian animals. The sixth plague caused boils to break out on the Egyptians, as well as their animals. This plagued demonstrated more of God's power over Egypt's gods by striking even the magicians. Beginning with the plague of gnats, the magicians had been unable to duplicate God's wonders. Now they could not even protect themselves from His power. Still, Pharaoh would not yield.

Third Cycle of Plagues and Final Plague

PLAGUE	INITIATION	RESULT	SCRIPTURE
Seven: Hail	Moses confronts Pharaoh in the morning	Storm destroys grain fields of the Egyptians	Exod. 9:13–35
Eight: Locusts	Moses goes to Pharaoh	Infestation of locusts strips the land of Egypt of plant life	Exod. 10:1–20
Nine: Darkness	Plague is unannounced	A deep darkness covers the land of Egypt for three days	Exod. 10:21–29
Ten: Death of the Firstborn	Moses gives his final warning to Pharaoh	The firstborn of every Egyptian family dies	Exod. 11:1—12:30

Plague Seven: Hail (9:13–35)

Round three of the conflicts likewise consisted of three plagues: hail, locusts, and darkness. Before sending hail, the Lord asserted that He alone is the Lord of history. Pharaoh probably did not realize or consider that in suffering the plagues he had actually experienced God's mercy. By now God could have totally

"He destroyed their vines with hail and their sycamore-figs with sleet. He gave over their cattle to the hail, their livestock to bolts of lightning" (Ps. 78:47–48).

25

destroyed all of Egypt. But He had raised up Pharaoh for the express purpose of demonstrating His mighty power and proclaiming His holy name (9:16).

With this seventh plague, God dealt more directly with the Egyptians. Again He gave them a one-day warning, but with the warning God offered the Egyptians themselves a chance to escape the effects of the plague (9:19). Indeed, some of the Pharaoh's officials "feared the word of the Lord" and heeded the warning (9:20). Some Egyptians were beginning to recognize God's power.

Unfortunately, many Egyptians still did not accept Moses' God. They were struck by the worst hail storm to hit Egypt in its history as a nation (9:24). Again the Israelites were spared.

The devastation of the plague forced Pharaoh to admit, "I have sinned" (9:27). He did not actually repent, though, and after the storm had stopped he again hardened his heart. At least he had made an admission of guilt, confessing, "I and my people are in the wrong" (9:27).

- *Pharaoh recognized his own guilt but needed*
- *to realize something more about himself.*
- *What God was trying to communicate to*
- *Pharaoh was that not only did the Hebrew*
- *slaves belong to God, but so did the land of*
- *Egypt and Pharaoh himself!*

QUESTIONS TO GUIDE YOUR STUDY

1. Why did God not end the conflict quickly by killing Pharaoh and any other

ruling Egyptian who refused to set the people free?

2. In what ways was God showing mercy to the Egyptians, in spite of their oppression of His people?

3. How did Pharaoh show that he was less understanding of spiritual matters than even his officials?

EXODUS 10 · · · · · · · · · · · · · · · · · · ·

Freeing Israel from slavery was not the primary purpose of the plagues. Rather, through these events generations of Israelites would come to know the Lord and His saving power.

Plague Eight: Locusts (10:1–20)

In instructing Moses concerning the eighth plague, the Lord announced the purpose of these signs and wonders. The plagues were not aimed merely at gaining Israel's release, but also at demonstrating God's sovereignty.

The demands on Pharaoh were increasing. As Moses and Aaron approached him again, the question was: How long would he refuse to humble himself before their God? (10:3). For the king of Egypt, who was thought to be a god himself, to bow to the God of his slaves was unthinkable. But the suffering caused by the preceding seven plagues should have made the unthinkable now thinkable.

The locust plague would finish what the hail plague had started. The barley and flax, which were ready for harvest at the time of the hailstorm, had been destroyed. Wheat and spelt, which had not sprouted at that time, would

Pharaoh accused Moses and the Israelites of plotting evil against Egypt (10:10). Certainly, Pharaoh knew in his heart that such was not true. How often do we attempt to avoid real issues by imagining situations that are of little probability? How often do we see things the way we want them to be rather than the way they really are?

now be devoured by swarms of locusts (9:31–32).

Negotiations Continue. Some of Pharaoh's officials had already heeded Moses' warnings during the last plague (9:20). For this plague they became bolder, urging Pharaoh to let the Hebrew people go. They had had enough; their Egypt was in ruins.

Pharaoh attempted another compromise. Moses could lead the people away to worship the Lord, but only the men could go (10:10–11). By retaining the women and children, Pharaoh knew that the worshipers would return; and he would keep his slaves. Obviously Moses was not agreeable to such terms, and negotiations broke down.

The devastation of the locusts caused Pharaoh once more to admit guilt and to confess, "I have sinned" (10:16). Inwardly, though, he had not changed; and when the locusts were gone his heart remained hardened.

Egyptian religion included a great number of gods. Many were personifications of the enduring natural forces in Egypt, such as the sun (Re or Atum), sky (Nut), and earth (Geb). The plague of darkness was a stinging strike against the power of Egypt's sun god. The Lord literally turned out this false deity's lights!

■ *Plague by plague Egypt was being ruined,*
■ *and yet Pharaoh ignored pleas from his own*
■ *officials to release the people. Such a stub-*
■ *born attitude, defiantly rejecting God's will,*
■ *is described appropriately as "hardening*
■ *the heart."*

Plague Nine: Darkness (10:21–29)

The ninth plague was a direct attack upon the king of Egypt's gods—the sun god. Ancient Egyptians worshiped the sun as the god Re, but the Lord showed His power to be greater. All of Egypt was plunged into total darkness except for where the Israelites lived. The sun god had been so utterly defeated that the darkness could "be felt" (10:21).

Pharaoh was ready to negotiate again, offering another compromise: he would now let all the people go, requiring that only their livestock and animals remain. Moses would not accept such terms, since the animals would be needed as sacrifices in worship. His offers rejected, Pharaoh angrily closed negotiations with Moses.

■ *The two negotiators parted. One of them was*
■ *pressured to his limits, full of anger, and out*
■ *of control. The other, fully in control, knew*
■ *he had done all he could.*

QUESTIONS TO GUIDE YOUR STUDY

1. Why is it so important to tell our children about our experiences with God?

2. Pharaoh accused Moses of plotting evil. Did Pharaoh actually believe that? Or was he in some way being deceptive with Moses?

3. Pharaoh ordered Moses out of his presence forever. Why does anger cause us to say things we will regret later when we have cooled off?

EXODUS 11 · · · · · · · · · · · · · · · ·

Time and again Moses had gone to Pharaoh with God's demands, only to be disappointed by Pharaoh's resistance. But now God announced "one more plague" that would have

The Firstborn

For every newly married couple, the first son born was believed to represent the prime of human vigor. Jacob described his firstborn son, Reuben, as "my might, the first sign of my strength" (Gen. 49:3). The final plague was the ultimate blow to the Egyptians, taking from them "the firstfruits of all their manhood" (Ps. 105:36).

a much different result; indeed, Pharaoh would drive the Israelites away.

The Final Plague (11:1–10)

The fourth and deciding round of the conflict consisted of only one final plague—the death of the firstborn of every family in Egypt. This plague would distinguish between the death of Egypt's firstborn and the preservation of Israel's firstborn.

In the last speech to Pharaoh, Moses described the approaching plague in graphic detail. The Egyptians would wail more loudly than they ever had before or ever would again. Egypt's officials would beg Moses to leave Egypt. In spite of Moses' passionate words of warning, Pharaoh's heart was still hardened and Moses left in anger.

■ *Moses had confronted Pharaoh repeatedly,*
■ *demanding he let Israel go. For six of the first*
■ *nine plagues, he had warned Pharaoh of the*
■ *suffering that would come if he refused to*
■ *free the people. Pharaoh's offerings of com-*
■ *promise must have tempted Moses to accept*
■ *and end the struggle. But Moses had a call*
■ *from God and could not.*

QUESTIONS TO GUIDE YOUR STUDY

1. How many opportunities to avoid the plagues did Pharaoh pass up? Is it possible to exhaust God's patience through our disobedience?

2. Why did Pharaoh's officials and the Egyptian people react differently to Moses than

"Egypt was glad when they left, because dread of Israel had fallen on them" (Ps. 105:38).

did Pharaoh himself? Does pride keep us from accepting God's sovereignty?

EXODUS 12 ·················

Pivotal to the Exodus event and the Passover observance was the offering of a lamb from the sheep or from the goats. This lamb's blood would substitute for the blood of Israel's first-born sons, saving them from the destroying angel.

THE EXODUS FROM EGYPT (12:1–51)

The last plague is the setting for what became Israel's central religious celebration—the Passover and Feast of Unleavened Bread.

Instructions for Passover (12:1–13)

The Book of Exodus alternates narrative accounts of God's dramatic saving event with instructions applicable to this event as well as to the ongoing worship of Israel. In the month of Abib Israel would observe Passover, for it was the month of the Exodus deliverance (12:2; 13:3–4).

God's instructions were specific as to how Israel should eat the Lord's Passover. On the tenth day of the month, they would select the animal to be sacrificed. On the fourteenth day, they would slaughter the animal and eat at evening. None of the animal was to be left over the following morning (Exod. 34:25).

A significant part of the Passover ritual was the daubing of blood from the sacrificed animal on the top and the two sides of the door frame. When the angel passed through, destroying the firstborn in Egypt, he would pass by the houses

The First Month

The name of the Hebrews' first month was Abib (12:2; 13:4), a name meaning "ears of grain." It was appropriately named since it was a harvest month, covering parts of our March and April. When the Jews returned from the Babylonian Exile, they brought with them the names of the Babylonian calendar. The Babylonians also counted the new year from the spring, and the Babylonian name *Nisan* (Esth. 3:7) eventually replaced the Hebrew name *Abib*.

that were marked in this fashion. This climactic strike against Egypt would execute the Lord's judgment on the gods of Egypt (12:12).

■ *The Hebrew slaves were to eat the Passover*
■ *"in haste" and dress themselves as if they*
■ *would be leaving Egypt immediately*
■ *(12:11). We exercise a strong faith when we*
■ *prepare for God to consummate those prom-*
■ *ises that have seemed most improbable.*

Feast of Unleavened Bread (12:14–20)

The Passover was also called the Feast of Unleavened Bread (12:17) because only unleavened bread was eaten during the seven days immediately following Passover (13:6–7). Unleavened bread signified the people's hasty departure from Egypt which allowed them no time to put leaven in their bread.

The First Passover Observance (12:21–28)

Moses assembled the elders of the people, giving them detailed instructions on how to prepare for that evening. The Lord would pass through Egypt, and "the destroyer" (12:23)—the supernatural agent of God's judgment—would strike. The Israelites would be protected by the blood on their door frames.

Unleavened Bread

The Feast of Unleavened Bread continued for seven days after the Passover. By eating unleavened bread during this week, the participants remembered the departure from Egypt, made so hastily that the people had no time to wait for bread to rise with leaven.

■ *The elders who had once griped about Moses'*
■ *leadership now carried out his instructions*
■ *for the Passover. They had been given new*
■ *hope. Again they envisioned the future in the*
■ *Promised Land, where they would celebrate*
■ *these new rituals.*

Plague Ten: Death of the Firstborn (12:29–36)

God killed the firstborn of every Egyptian family, passing over the Israelite families. At last, Pharaoh was forced to recognize the superiority of Moses' God over all the gods of Egypt and over himself as well. In his first meeting with Moses, Pharaoh had stated defiantly, "I do not know the LORD" (5:2). Now he knew the Lord and could only plead humbly of Moses, "Also bless me" (12:32).

In the agony of this death scene, the Egyptians drove the Israelites out of Egypt. Relations among Moses, Aaron, and the Egyptians changed significantly as a result of the last plague. Moses had gained great respect among Pharaoh's officials (11:3). Following Moses' instructions (11:2), the Israelites took silver, gold, and clothing from the Egyptians. This plundering of Egypt's wealth was actually necessary, since as slaves the Hebrews would not have had the resources to survive a wilderness journey.

- *The plagues eventually resulted in Israel's*
- *freedom. The central purpose of the plagues,*
- *however, was the revelation of God. Pharaoh*
- *and the Egyptians, as well as Moses and the*
- *Israelites, came to know the Lord through*
- *the events of these mighty works.*

Regulations for the Passover (12:43–51)

The narrative again switches to instructions that would pertain to Israel's new life in their new land. They had been slaves and foreigners in Egypt. In the future they would be settled in

Number of Hebrews in the Exodus?

Exodus 12:37 is usually translated so that the number of Hebrews departing Egypt was six hundred thousand men. Adding women and children would bring the total number of people to around two million. This number seems excessively large, raising questions as to how Egypt could have maintained control of such a massive group of people. Some note that the Hebrew word *'eleph,* usually translated "thousand," can also be translated as "clan" or "fighting unit," so that the actual number in the Exodus could have been less than the traditional six hundred thousand. We may not know the exact number of those who left in the Exodus, but we do know that such an event happened as a saving act of God.

their own land, and others in their midst would be the slaves and foreigners. Regulations for future Passovers must cover these new circumstances.

In terms of its redemptive effects, none of the daily sacrifices made throughout the Old Testament were as dramatic as the Passover sacrifice. This most important Israelite feast would commemorate for years to come God's deliverance of His people from Egyptian bondage.

QUESTIONS TO GUIDE YOUR STUDY

1. How did the Passover lamb function as a substitute?
2. Why is the Passover observance similar to the Lord's Supper for Christians?
3. Why is Pharaoh's request, "Bless me," such a contrast to his query, "Who is the LORD?" when he first met Moses?

EXODUS 13

Celebrations such as the Feast of Unleavened Bread and ceremonies like the consecration of the firstborn would be memorials to what God accomplished in the Exodus. These perpetual reminders would encourage future generations to understand God's saving acts.

CONSECRATION OF THE FIRSTBORN (13:1–16)

In memory of the death of Egypt's firstborn, all the firstborn of Israel, both humans and animals, belonged to the Lord (13:2, 15). He had spared them when He decimated the families of Egypt. Throughout their history as a people, Israel attached unusual value to the eldest son and assigned special privileges and responsibilities to him.

Jewish people have followed the command of Exod. 13:16 quite literally. The story of the Exodus redemption did become for them, as instructed, "a sign on your hand and a symbol on your forehead." Scripture passages from Exod. 13 and Deut. 6 and 11, written on small scrolls, are placed in leather containers, which are then fastened to the forehead and left arm.

- *A primary function of the Hebrew family was*
- *the teaching of religion. Even today children*
- *should be able to ask at home, "What does this*
- *mean?" and receive the proper spiritual*
- *instruction and guidance. Parents have more*
- *influence over children than any other adults.*

GOD'S GUIDING, PROVIDING, PROTECTING PRESENCE (13:17–18:27)

The first section of Exodus (Exod. 1:1–13:16) focused on God's powerful, saving presence and built steadily to a dramatic conclusion—the death of Egypt's firstborn and Israel's Exodus. The second section (Exod. 13:17–18:27) likewise focused on God's presence, which guided, provided, and protected on the journey to Mount Sinai.

Joseph's Bones

Joseph rose to a position of great power in Egypt, second in command to Pharaoh. But Egypt was not Joseph's home. Nearing death, he made the Hebrews promise to carry his bones back to Canaan, for he knew that God would return them to the Promised Land (Gen. 50:24–25). Moses was able to fulfill that vow (Exod. 13:19).

Exit from Egypt (13:17–22)

By means of the pillars of cloud and fire, the Lord guided Israel from Succoth to the wilderness of Etham.

The God who had saved the Israelites from slavery was now guiding, leading, and protecting them. They had armed themselves in the event they were attacked on the way; but the Lord, in His wisdom, directed them away from the route where fighting was most likely to occur. Instead, they traveled toward the Red Sea.

■ *Israel would long remember God's*
■ *protecting cloud. One of the psalms*
■ *recalls how God answered their*
■ *prayers: "He spoke to them from the pillar of*
■ *cloud" (Ps. 99:7).*

Glory

The basic meaning of the Hebrew word for *glory* is "heavy in weight." The "glory" that God would gain through the Exodus event (14:4) refers to the weighty importance of His presence. Both Israel and Egypt would recognize the importance of the Lord, the weight He carries among all creatures.

EXODUS 14

The natural and supernatural combined at the Red Sea to produce God's deliverance of His people from the grip of Pharaoh's army.

Pharaoh Pursues His Slaves (14:1–9)

As Moses led the people into the wilderness, Pharaoh again wanted his slaves and led his armies after them. Where Israel was camped made them appear to be boxed in by the sea to the east, the deserts to the north and south, and the advancing Egyptian armies to the west.

What was about to take place was that God would "gain glory" (14:4). Every event had the purpose of revealing God to the people of Israel and Egypt. Israel would experience God as a redeeming Savior. Egypt would experience Him as a powerful deity. Once more the Lord hardened the heart of Pharaoh so that through his defeat Egypt would realize that the Lord is God (14:18).

■ *Israel's turning back led Pharaoh to believe*
■ *they were confused and lost. Little did he*
■ *know that their wandering was part of God's*
■ *divine plan.*

Victory at the Sea (14:10–31)

The miracle at the Red Sea became the greatest moment in Israel's history—the moment God created a nation for Himself by delivering them from one of the military superpowers of that time.

Pharaoh had assembled armies of chariots. His military objective was to move fast, overtake the Hebrews, and return them, by force, to Egypt. Yet all of this military strategy had not accounted for Egypt's real opponent—Israel's God.

The Hebrews had marched boldly from Egypt (14:8). One sighting of the pursuing Egyptians, however, sapped their confidence, as well as their belief in God's power to deliver. While Pharaoh's objective was to regain the Hebrews' slave services (14:5), the Hebrews themselves imagined that he intended to kill them (14:12).

For a tense night the presence of the Lord guarded Israel from the armies of Egypt. Then the Lord, in one of the most marvelous redemptive acts of Old Testament times, opened up the

Seeing Is Believing

The Israelites easily trusted God when they saw what He did to Pharaoh at the Red Sea (14:31). Why must we wait for visible demonstrations before we trust ourselves to God's care? Jesus challenges us to believe even though we "have not seen" (John 20:29).

sea. God led His people through the divided waters of the sea and then flooded the sea again as the Egyptians tried to follow.

What the final plague failed to accomplish, the Red Sea miracle did. The Egyptians finally realized they could not defy the God who fought for Israel, but their realization came too late (14:25). The Israelites witnessed an extraordinary event, crossing the sea safely on dry ground while their enemies perished. Finally, they trusted the Lord and Moses who represented Him (14:31).

- *An air of mystery surrounds the Red Sea*
- *event. We do not know precisely where the*
- *sea crossing occurred. We do not know who*
- *or how many may have been involved. What*
- *we do know is that God was at work.*

QUESTIONS TO GUIDE YOUR STUDY

1. When you feel trapped or find yourself in a situation that offers no way out, how can you practice trusting in God to provide "dry ground" for your anxious feet?
2. Why does God perform saving actions, even at times when His people have failed to trust?
3. Why should we store up memories of those occasions when God has delivered us from some trouble or difficulty?

EXODUS 15

Hebrew poetry is not like modern Western poetry. Nevertheless, Hebrew writers could use the imagery and tone of poetic form to impress God's message upon His people. Chapter 15 is the only part of the Book of Exodus written in poetry.

THE SONGS OF MOSES AND MIRIAM (15:1–21)

For generations after the Red Sea event, Israel commemorated its salvation by singing the triumphant songs of Moses and Miriam. These songs were hymns that praised the Lord as the sovereign God and Savior.

The Song of Moses (15:1–18)

The Song of Moses begins with the same words which make up the Song of Miriam. The Lord is exalted for defeating the Egyptians in the sea (15:1, 21).

The Character of the Lord (15:2–3, 11–12)

The gratitude of the Israelites expressed itself in the form of praise. When God's people meditated on the redemption their God had provided, the natural response was to praise Him. One aspect of that praise was to reflect on His true character. The song states several things about the unique nature of Israel's God.

My strength. The Lord was the source of strength.

My song. The Lord had given them a reason to sing.

My salvation. The Lord had delivered them physically from slavery and death; He would also deliver them spiritually.

My God. They had personally experienced this God.

Redeem

The legal and commercial activities of the ancient business world provided biblical writers with one of the most basic and dynamic images for describing God's saving activity toward humankind. The concept of *redeeming* grows out of the custom of buying back something which formerly belonged to the purchaser but for some reason had passed into ownership of another. The original owner could regain ownership by paying a redemption price for it. The image of *redeeming* is prominent in Exodus: at the sea God redeemed His people from Egyptian slavery (15:13).

My father's God. This was the God who had appeared to their ancestors, the patriarchs.

A warrior. The Lord was the one who fought for them.

Majestic in holiness. The Lord inspired awe and fear.

Awesome in glory. Israel recognized the honor and importance of the Lord.

Working wonders. Events had unmistakably demonstrated the immediate and powerful action of the Lord.

Among the gods. Of all the deities worshiped in that ancient world, there was only one for Israel; and His name is the Lord.

■ *God is not simply the greatest of many*
■ *gods—He is the only true God. God is the liv-*
■ *ing God, which separates Him from all other*
■ *gods and idols.*

Recounting the Deliverance (15:4–10)

In their singing, Israel affirmed that the victory over the Egyptians was entirely God's doing. The miracle at the Red Sea was not treated merely as a natural event or as Israel's victory alone. Their salvation was the result of God at work.

Looking to the Future (15:13–17)

In the aftermath of so great a victory and so tremendous a deliverance, Israel was able to trust completely in the Lord's power to bring them to the land He had promised. At this point, their faith envisioned many more victories to come.

The New King (15:18)

The song closes with a shout of the Lord's eternal reign. For years the Israelites had served the king of Egypt. Now they would serve another king—the Lord, who would reign forever.

■   *Moses' song employs the vivid images*
■   *and style of ancient Near Eastern*
■   *mythical poetry. Yet this song does so*
■ *in order to communicate the awesome maj-*
■ *esty of the Lord and His dominion over*
■ *His foes.*

The Song of Miriam (15:19–21)

Miriam, the sister of Moses and Aaron, had played a key role in the rescue of Moses (2:4–8). Now, after crossing the Red Sea, she assumed the role of prophetess and led the women in the song of victory that sprung from faith and gratitude (15:20–21). Her song was possibly the earliest recorded response to the Red Sea event.

■   *The service we render to God may*
■   *sometimes be remembered long after*
■   *we have gone. Many years after Mir-*
■ *iam's time, she was still remembered by the*
■ *prophet Micah as one of the leaders of the*
■ *Exodus (Mic. 6:4).*

A DOUBTING, COMPLAINING PEOPLE

The journey from the Red Sea to Mount Sinai was filled with miracles, through which God provided water, quails, and manna. All this occurred in spite of Israel's complaining insubordination.

The Prophetess

Miriam is one of only nine women who are identified in the Bible as a prophetess (the others being Deborah, Huldah, Noadiah, Anna, and Philip's four daughters). All these women were God's spokespersons, but their ministries varied greatly. In Miriam's case, the Holy Spirit inspired prophecy in the form of song, as Miriam called upon Israel to celebrate God's deliverance (15:20).

The Test of Thirst (15:22–27)

After celebrating their deliverance in song and dance, Israel followed Moses into the wilderness, but soon the difficult wilderness life proved too hard. The first point on the Israelites' journey after crossing the Red Sea was the Desert of Shur, a region on Egypt's northeastern border. Three days of travel without water had caused the people to forget about the marvelous feat of deliverance at the sea and to focus on their discomfort.

At the next stop in the desert, Marah, the people found water. But this site was typical of pools of water in the Sinai peninsula: the water was bitter and undrinkable. Indeed, it was precisely because of the bitter water that the place was named "Marah," which in Hebrew means "bitter" (15:23).

The people now complained to Moses because of their need for fresh water. Their faith was already cracking. Moses called on the Lord. God answered Moses' prayer by telling him to cast a branch from a tree into the water. The people witnessed the provision of God as the water became sweet and drinkable. Although the people had chosen to grumble rather than to trust, God delivered them from their difficult circumstances.

The relationship between God and Israel was based on a covenant similar to the political and economic agreements commonly made between nations of the ancient Near East. Even before reaching Mount Sinai, God established a law with Israel. Their obligation would be to obey His commands; His obligation would be to protect them from the plagues that struck Egypt. God promised healing to His people.

With the first test in the wilderness, the lack of water, Israel had been both untrusting and impatient. Had they just continued moving forward, believing that God would provide, they would have come to Elim. Elim's exact location is unknown, but its description implies an abundance of drinking water. The twelve wells and seventy palm trees at Elim made it a perfect place to camp.

70 Palm Trees

The Israelites were in need of refreshment as they arrived at Elim, and they found it. While their thirst was satisfied by twelve springs, another treat was supplied by the seventy palm trees. The date palm, among the earliest of cultivated trees, was characteristic of oases and watered places. Its fruit is highly valued by desert travelers since it may be consumed fresh or dried or made into cakes for a portable and easily storable food.

- *The real need at this stage of the journey was*
- *not for God to work a miracle at Marah, but*
- *for the people to trust God until they reached*
- *Elim. They failed the first test of faith. How*
- *often do we grumble about circumstances*
- *when God's solution lies just ahead?*

QUESTIONS TO GUIDE YOUR STUDY

1. Why are songs and music an effective way to express our joy and thanksgiving?

2. What is the connection between obeying God and receiving God's healing?

3. Why does God sometimes answer His people's requests, even when they grumble against His leaders?

EXODUS 16

Israel needed to realize that the saving God of the Red Sea would be the providing God of the desert. Learning about the true character of God should not have been the long, slow process that it was.

"I Will Test Them"

God tests the loyalty of His people. Abraham's loyalty to God was tested when the patriarch was asked to sacrifice his son Isaac (Gen. 22:1). The Israelites were tested when God instructed them on how to gather manna (Exod. 16:4–5). Jesus tested His disciple Philip concerning how to feed the multitude (John 6:5–7). As Jesus' disciples, we too will be tested to determine the level of our faith in Christ. Such testing is not difficult when we respond in trust and obedience.

EATING MANNA AND QUAIL (16:1–36)

God provided food for His people, causing it to appear at the right time and place to meet their needs.

The Test of Hunger (16:1–5)

The next point on the journey was the Desert of Sin, a barren region somewhere west of the Sinai plateau on the Sinai peninsula. At Marah the people had been thirsty and God supplied water for their need. Facing a new test—this time hunger—they could have looked to God with positive anticipation of how He would meet their need. Yet they failed another test of their faith, grumbling instead to Moses and Aaron.

The Israelites' grumbling reveals just how fragile their faith was. They recalled the food they had enjoyed in Egypt, forgetting how miserable their lot had been as slaves. Worse, they actually thought God might let them die of starvation (16:3). A strong faith would have been continually praising God for redeeming them from slavery and trusting Him to preserve their lives.

God announced a test for the people. He would provide food for them, but He would also see whether they would follow His instructions for gathering the food. If they could not be trusted to obey in small matters, such as gathering food, how could they be trusted in much more important matters?

■ *God will supply us with everything we*
■ *need—but not necessarily with everything*
■ *we desire or want. We should trust God to*
■ *know how much we actually need of what*
■ *we want.*

Grumbling Against the LORD (16:6–9)

Moses clarified for the people what the real issue was. What was being tested was not the quality of Moses' and Aaron's leadership, but the degree to which the people would really trust their God. They had grumbled against Moses and Aaron, but in reality their grumbling was against the Lord. And equally important, He had heard their grumbling.

God Provides Meat and Bread (16:10–16)

In God's timing, the needs of the people for food were met.

The quail which visited the Hebrew camp were probably a migrating flock. Huge numbers of quail migrate north during the spring after wintering in Africa. When the fatigued birds stop to rest, they can be caught easily. God had already made provisions for meat, but the people grumbled before it was time for those provisions to go into effect.

Manna consisted of small, round grains or flakes, which appeared around the camp each morning with the dew. The flakes could be ground and baked into cakes or boiled. The name *manna* may have come from the question the Israelites asked in Hebrew when they first saw the flakes: *Man hu,*' meaning "What is it?" (16:15).

A Miracle of Timing

Both the quail and the manna that appeared in the Hebrew camp have been supposed by some to be natural events. The behavior of the quail represents the pattern of migrating flocks. Today a type of manna has been identified with the secretions left on tamarisk bushes by insects feeding on the sap. But we must remember three things: (1) We cannot be certain these events were completely natural; (2) the people themselves believed that God had caused the manna and quail to appear; (3) the supernatural miracle is that God set the time and place when they would appear.

■ *It is hard to determine whether the quail and*
■ *manna operated beyond or within the laws of*
■ *nature. Either way, God's miracle of provi-*
■ *sion was His providing the exact amount*
■ *needed on a regular daily schedule.*

The Test of Gathering (16:17–30)

This chapter of Exodus closes with a reminder to the reader: "An omer is one tenth of an ephah" (16:36). As a unit of dry measure, the omer was a little more than two quarts. An omer of manna was enough food for one person for one day (16:16).

The test for the people was to see whether they could trust God to provide their daily needs for food. If there were four people in a tent, that tent would need four omers of manna each day. The manna was gathered in the morning, and a gatherer must gather the full day's amount at that time, for the afternoon sun melted whatever flakes remained on the ground. All the manna gathered had to be eaten on that day, for any kept until the next morning became infested with maggots.

Of course, some disobeyed the instructions, attempting to save a portion of manna for the following day; and it turned to maggots. The instructions changed, however, on the sixth day. They were then to gather twice the amount—two omers per person—in order to have enough manna for two days. The manna that was kept until the seventh day would be edible, not infested with maggots. Again, some disobeyed these instructions, attempting to gather on the seventh day, but the attempt was futile.

The rest from manna gathering on the seventh day began an observance that would become a major part of the people's worship of the Lord. The example for this special day of rest had been established by God's rest on the seventh day after creation. It was to be considered a holy day (16:23).

- *God's tests of obedience are also tests of sin.*
- *To disobey God consciously and deliberately*
- *is sinful behavior that tarnishes our life*
- *of faith.*

The Jar of Manna (16:31–36)

The people had demonstrated their inability to sustain faith. As a reminder to them of God's providing care, Aaron preserved an omer of manna in a jar, which would later be placed in the ark of the covenant (called "the testimony"). God did not fail His people, supplying manna for the entire forty years they were in the wilderness.

QUESTIONS TO GUIDE YOUR STUDY

1. How many times did the people fail to follow the instructions for gathering manna?

2. Why are visual symbols of God's protective acts helpful as reminders of His goodness to us?

3. Why was it important for the people to rest on the Sabbath from their food gathering?

"Behind the second curtain was a room called the Most Holy Place, which had the golden altar of incense and the gold-covered ark of the covenant. This ark contained the gold jar of manna, Aaron's staff that had budded, and the stone tablets of the covenant" (Heb. 9:3–4).

EXODUS 17

Even after God had supplied their food and drink, the people still cried for the good old days of Egypt. Nevertheless, the providing God would now reveal Himself as a protecting God against the Amalekites.

Testing God

In his last speeches to the people, Moses reminded them of the incident at Massah, warning them, "Do not test the LORD your God" (Deut. 6:16). Jesus emphasized Moses' warning when He quoted it to Satan while being tempted (Matt. 4:7). In spite of warnings by the two most prominent teachers of the Bible, people still do test God. Do we not realize that our testing of God shows our lack of faith, as well as our unwillingness truly to obey?

Moses renamed Rephidim "Meribah," which in Hebrew means "quarreling."

Doubting People Test God's Presence (17:1–7)

The last stop for the Hebrews before they reaching Mount Sinai was the site of Rephidim, somewhere near the base of the mountain. They were once again in need of drinking water. Their first response was to complain against Moses.

God had met the needs of His people in each of the previous crises. When they were thirsty at Marah, He made bitter water turn sweet. When they were hungry in the Desert of Sin, he brought quail at the right time and manna day by day. Unfortunately, these extraordinary experiences had not changed a people of weak faith.

At Rephidim the lack of water not only resulted in grumbling. This time emotions flared as the people quarreled with Moses. Their demands for water were so intense that Moses feared they would stone him (17:4).

The people's faith in the protecting hand of God was actually falling apart. Not only did they still fear dying (17:3); they even questioned whether God was still present with them (17:7). Moses chose another name, "Massah," meaning "testing," as a reminder that Israel had tested God with their disobedience.

Once more God provided in spite of the people's lack of trust. The miracle of bringing water from a rock was granted with two requirements: Moses was to use the same staff that he had used in Egypt to strike the Nile River, and he was to perform the deed before the elders of Israel. Maybe the elders would remember what the Lord did in Egypt when Moses raised that staff and thus place their trust in their God.

- *Even though the people may resist spiritual*
- *leadership, God will stand by the leader who*
- *remains loyal and obedient to Him.*

Cursing the Amalekites (17:8–15)

The Amalekites were a nomadic tribe of formidable strength. In fact, they were the first hostile and savage desert tribe to attack the Israelites as they journeyed from Egypt.

Joshua was born in Egypt during the period of slavery. Natural leadership abilities that would have remained undeveloped for an Egyptian slave now blossomed for this free young man. As Israel was forced to defend themselves against the Amalekites, Joshua served as Moses' general.

The battle demonstrated a people and their God working together. Joshua led the troops in the actual fighting. God was not going to eliminate the enemy without effort being exerted by the Israelites themselves. On the other hand, Israel could not win without the Lord. The course of the battle was in Israel's favor only while Moses raised his hands to the Lord—an action symbolizing the release of God's power on Israel's behalf. When Moses grew tired, Aaron and Hur held up his hands until the battle was won.

Israel won this initial battle against Amalek; but fighting between these two peoples would continue, even after Israel settled in Canaan. Both a written scroll and an altar would continually remind the Israelites that they had divine help in war—the Lord would forever fight with them.

The Amalekites

The descendants of Amalek, the grandson of Esau (Gen. 36:12), inhabited the desolate wasteland of the northeast Sinai peninsula and the Negev. Though they lost the initial battle against Israel, they continued to wage a barbaric guerrilla war against them (Deut. 25:17–18). Their atrocities against Israel were not forgotten, and were finally avenged by the tribe of Simeon (1 Chron. 4:42–43).

- *The Amalekites blocked Israel's path to*
- *Mount Sinai, a destination they could not be*
- *denied. Hur helped Aaron hold Moses' hands*
- *up so Israel could prevail. Christian leaders*
- *are similarly in need of support from Chris-*
- *tian followers if the church is to move for-*
- *ward as a force for God.*

QUESTIONS TO GUIDE YOUR STUDY

1. What did the people do that "tested" the Lord? What do we do today to test God?
2. How can we "hold up the hands" of our pastors and church leaders?

EXODUS 18 · · · · · · · · · · · · · · · · · · ·

Moses's father-in-law became his teacher, showing Moses how to be an effective leader and administrator without burning himself out.

DELEGATING LEADERSHIP TASKS (18:1–27)

When heavy administrative burdens threatened to overwhelm Moses, his father-in-law Jethro instructed him about how the task could be better distributed.

The Family Reunites (18:1–12)

In a flashback, the book of Exodus updates us on Moses' family. Previously his first son, Gershom, was introduced (2:22; 4:24–25). Gershom's name sounds like the Hebrew words for "an alien there," reflecting Moses' experience after fleeing Egypt and becoming a foreigner in Midian. The name of Moses' second son,

Eliezer, means "my God is my helper," which appropriately reflects God's deliverance of Moses from Pharaoh.

Moses' wife, Zipporah, accompanied him to Egypt, taking Gershom with them. Eliezer was probably born in Egypt, but it appears that Zipporah and the two boys returned to stay with her father until Moses had led the people out of Egypt. Now, as the Israelites camped near Mount Sinai, Moses' father-in-law, Jethro, reunited the family.

Of particular interest is that Jethro was a Midianite priest, and the deity whom he served is not explicitly identified. As Moses related all the Lord had done in delivering Israel from the Egyptians, Jethro praised Israel's God. His praise turned into a confession of faith, exclaiming, "The LORD is greater than all other gods" (18:11).

■ *Family members strengthen one another*
■ *spiritually by sharing together their experi-*
■ *ences of God. We can influence our family in*
■ *much the same way that Moses' testimony*
■ *led Jethro to praise God.*

Effective Administration (18:13–27)

One man can only do so much. Moses was suffering fatigue from the immense responsibilities he carried. A wise father-in-law diagnosed the problem and offered a solution. At Jethro's recommendation, Moses appointed judges to handle most of the disputes among the people. Moses himself would continue to teach and lead as God's representative, judging only the complex cases. This simple delegation of authority

Moses' Father-in-Law

Some uncertainty exists in the Bible concerning the identity of Moses' father-in-law. Three different names are described with the Hebrew word for "father-in-law."

Reuel is named as the "father" (Exod. 2:18, 21) of Zipporah, Moses' wife. He is called a "priest of Midian" (Exod. 2:16) and described as "Moses' father-in-law" (Num. 10:29). Jethro, like Reuel, is called "the priest of Midian" and described as Moses' "father-in-law" (Exod. 3:1)

Hobab is called "the son of Reuel the Midianite" (Num. 10:29), but is also described with the Hebrew word for "father-in-law" (Judg. 4:11).

This Hebrew word could have a more general meaning of "related by marriage," and in Judg. 4:11 might mean "brother-in-law." Possibly, then, Hobab was Moses' brother-in-law, while Reuel and Jethro were different names for the same person.

relieved Moses' day-to-day work load; greater responsibilities of a different nature lay ahead for Israel's leader.

■ *Jethro's contributions were more significant*
■ *than may appear. If Moses' ability to lead*
■ *had been seriously weakened by fatigue, the*
■ *approaching mission at Mount Sinai might*
■ *have been jeopardized.*

QUESTIONS TO GUIDE YOUR STUDY

1. Why would Moses not have wanted his family in Egypt while he confronted Pharaoh?

2. Should we wait until we have witnessed God's actions for ourselves before we praise Him? How important is it for us to listen as others testify concerning their experiences of God?

3. Can we become so enthusiastic about serving God that we attempt to do too much too soon?

Travelogue

The journey to Mount Sinai took about two months: first month, fifteenth day—leave Egypt (12:2,51); second month, fifteenth day—arrive Desert of Sin (16:1); third month—arrive Desert of Sinai (19:1).

EXODUS 19 . . . .

The third section of the Book of Exodus, Exod. 19:1–24:18, focuses on the demanding presence of God. At Mount Sinai God would reveal the way He expected His people to live, a way of holiness—to serve as priests among the nations.

GOD COVENANTS WITH HIS PEOPLE (19:1–25)

While God was executing the plagues on Egypt, Moses again and again demanded that Pharaoh release the people in order that they might worship the Lord. At last the moment of worship and service had arrived. At Sinai Israel was to commit itself to the Lord in covenant.

A Kingdom of Priests (19:1–8)

Moses stood with the people in their camp in front of the mountain. Undoubtedly he recalled the Lord's words at the burning bush, "You will worship God on this mountain" (3:12). The first task was finished; Moses had led the people out of Egypt. The second task would begin on this mountain, and Moses started his climb up.

The Lord based His call to covenant commitment on His mighty acts of deliverance. In spite of His people's disobedience, He had carried them "on eagles' wings" (19:4) from Egypt, through the Red Sea, through thirst and hunger in the desert, and over enemy armies. But their redemption was linked with God's demand for obedience.

Only through obedience to God's covenant could Israel fill its role as "a kingdom of priests and a holy nation" (19:5–6). In that role Israel would serve God as His mediators with the rest of the world. The people accepted God's terms unconditionally (19:8), but could they sustain this level of commitment? Moses ascended Mount Sinai again to solemnize the arrangement.

■ When God desires to covenant with us, offering us a unique role in His divine plan, we
■ must be motivated to answer as did Israel:
■ "We will do everything the LORD has said."

Sinai and Horeb

Sinai was a mountain in the south central part of a peninsula in the northwestern end of Arabia. The term *Horeb* is often used to refer to Sinai in such a way as to make the two names synonymous (3:1). Since Horeb means "waste" or "wilderness area," it seems best to consider Horeb as the general term for the area and Sinai as the specific peak where God manifested Himself to Moses.

The modern name for the traditional site of Sinai is Jebel Musa (meaning "the mount of Moses"). Jebel Musa, one of three granite peaks near the southern tip of the peninsula, rises to a height of 7,500 feet. Other sites have been proposed for the mountain where Moses and Israel met God. While we are not sure of an exact location, we are sure of the many significant revelations God made of Himself there.

Preparing to Meet God (19:9–15)

Consecration refers to persons (or things) being separated to God. When persons were "consecrated," they were set apart to live according to God's demands and in His service. The activities of the people as they prepared for "the third day" (19:11) may have seemed strange, but they were to encounter a holy God; and they must take such a privilege seriously.

The Lord Descends (19:16–25)

The Lord came down, visiting the mountain with the thunder and lightning of His glorious presence. The physical appearance or personal manifestation of a god to a person or to people is known as *theophany*. While God does not reveal Himself to the ordinary sight of humans, at times He chooses to reveal Himself in theophanies.

The theophany at Mount Sinai was a terrifying experience. The day began with a thick cloud over the mountain, as well as the thunder and lightning. The Lord appeared in fire and smoke, and the mountain trembled, possibly resembling the movement of an earthquake; and the whole experience was accompanied by the blaring of a trumpet. The people thought that to actually see God could be fatal.

Moses warned the people to respect the holy (and potentially dangerous) presence of God on the mountain. Even Moses himself approached God only when He called (19:3, 20). The people could stand at the foot of the mountain, but they were not to touch the mountain itself. It was holy, sacred territory, set apart for the awesome presence of God.

Sinai's phenomena indicate volcanic
action—fire, smoke, quaking earth—but no
volcano is to be found in the Sinai peninsula.
The accompanying sounds of a trumpet and
the voice of God (19:19) added to the super-
natural character of this experience.

QUESTIONS TO GUIDE YOUR STUDY

1. How did God describe the manner in which He brought Israel out of Egypt?
2. This Sinai covenant and experience was not for Israel's benefit alone. How would other peoples become involved?
3. What procedures were the people to follow in preparing to meet with God?

EXODUS 20

After the Israelites arrived at Mount Sinai, God gave to His people the Ten Commandments (Exod. 20) and other laws central to the covenant (Exod. 21–23).

The Sinai covenant follows the form of the sovereign-vassal treaty that was well known in the ancient Near East. Such a treaty established the relationship between a superior power (the sovereign) and an inferior subject (the vassal). The parties involved were often a king and his servants, but the Sinai covenant would be between God and His people.

THE TEN COMMANDMENTS (20:1–17)

The Ten Commandments are God's covenant ground rules for life with Him. They are the basic policy statements which were to govern

"You Shall Not"

Two kinds of law can be found in the ancient Near East. One kind consists of broad categorical laws which set forth absolute principles. The Ten Commandments represent this kind of law. They do not specify how they are to be enforced or what penalties are to be invoked, but they do make unconditional commands that place moral obligations on us.

The Ten Commandments were not given only for the Hebrew people but they are also abiding laws for all of us today. They have an universal quality about them because they convey duties for everyone and reveal to us the basic morality required by God. Yet they are truly significant only when we are committed to the God behind them.

Israel's life in the covenant community with God. All of the commandments except commandments four and five (Exod. 20:8–11, 12) are prohibitions; they define negatively the covenant relationship between God and Israel.

Title of the Sovereign (20:1–2)

Sovereign-vassal treaties usually began with a royal title naming and identifying the king making the treaty. The first section of the Sinai covenant introduces the covenant maker: "I am the LORD your God" (20:2a). For the Israelites to accept the covenant, they had to accept the lordship of God.

Historical Prologue (20:2)

After identifying the treaty maker, a historical prologue then reviewed or outlined the past relationships between the two parties to the treaty. The purpose was to justify the new covenant, and a prologue often did this by emphasizing the gracious acts of the king. The Sinai covenant similarly describes God as the one "who brought you out of Egypt, out of the land of slavery." God's redemption of Israel from Egyptian slavery was the basis for His covenant with them.

The General Stipulations (20:3–17)

The treaty stipulations or agreements were presented in two parts. Part one was the primary agreement or obligation agreed to by the two parties. This part, known as the general stipulations, corresponds to the Ten Commandments of verses 3–17. Part two, which consisted of more specific stipulations, corresponds to the Book of the Covenant in Exod. 20:23–23:33.

Commandments Relating to God

COMMANDMENT	SCRIPTURE	JESUS' TEACHINGS
One: You shall have no other gods before me	Exod. 20:3; Deut. 5:7	Matt. 4:10; 6:33; 22:37–40
Two: You shall not make for yourself an idol	Exod. 20:4–6; Deut. 5:8–10	Matt. 6:24; Luke 16:13
Three: You shall not misuse the name of the Lord	Exod. 20:7; Deut. 5:11	Matt. 5:33–37; 6:9; 23:16–22
Four: Remember the Sabbath day by keeping it holy	Exod. 20:8–11; Deut. 5:12–15	Matt. 12:1–13; Mark 2:23–27; 3:1–6; Luke 6:1–11

Life with God (20:3–11).
The first four commandments are related to one's relationship with God.

No other gods (20:3). One of the great distinctives of Israel's religion (and of Judeo-Christian religion) is monotheism. Those who would worship the Lord must recognize and revere only one God. The first commandment thus differentiated Israel from its polytheistic pagan neighbors, who worshiped many gods.

No idols (20:4–6). The ancient Hebrews lived in a world filled with idols. Egyptians represented their deities in various human-animal forms, but Israel's religion must be different. The second commandment demanded an imageless worship. While this appears to be simply a negative statement concerning idols, it has positive implications. God desired *spiritual* worship from His people.

No misuse of God's name (20:7). God's name was known only because He chose to make it known. God is mysterious, lofty, and

Paul and the Commandments

Paul named several of the Ten Commandments while making his point that the Law should no longer be viewed legalistically. Like Jesus, he saw all the commandments summed up and fulfilled in the command to love (Rom. 13:9). But this love is much more than shallow emotions. Paul knew that only with the aid of the Spirit of God can we meet the requirement of love, which fulfills the Law (Gal. 5:14–18).

The Greatest Commandment

When Jesus was asked which commandment is the greatest, He did not answer with any of the Ten Commandments. Rather, He chose the two "love" commandments (Matt. 22:36–40). Incredibly, Jesus summed up the whole Law, as well as the teaching of the prophets, with two commandments. The two great principles of love for God and for neighbor should be the foundation of our Christian lives.

unapproachable; but He chose to bridge this gap with humankind by revealing His name. The divine name revealed God's power, authority, and holiness; thus, Israel must have great reverence for it. The third commandment prohibited any violation of God's name.

Observe the Sabbath (20:8–11). While the Israelites could work on six days, they were to cease work on the seventh day. The fourth commandment established the Sabbath as a day of rest, considered holy to the Lord. The reason given in Exod. 20:11 is that God's rest on the seventh day after creation made the day holy. A second reason for observing the Sabbath was as a reminder of the people's redemption from slavery in Egypt (Deut. 5:15).

A life guided by the Ten Commandments will not give another god credit for what the Lord has done, nor will it worship what human hands rather than the true God have made.

Commandments Relating to Others

COMMANDMENT	SCRIPTURE	JESUS' TEACHINGS
Five: Honor your father and your mother	Exod. 20:12; Deut. 5:16	Matt. 15:4–6; 19:19; Mark 7:9–13 Luke 18:20
Six: You shall not murder	Exod. 20:13; Deut. 5:17	Matt. 5:21–24; 19:18; Mark 10:19; Luke 18:20
Seven: You shall not commit adultery	Exod. 20:14; Deut. 5:18	Matt. 5:27–30; 19:18 Mark 10:19; Luke 18:20
Eight: You shall not steal	Exod. 20:15; Deut. 5:19	Matt. 19:18 Mark 10:19; Luke 18:20

Commandments Relating to Others

COMMANDMENT	SCRIPTURE	JESUS' TEACHINGS
Nine: You shall not give false testimony	Exod. 20:16; Deut. 5:20	Matt. 5:37; 19:18 Mark 10:19; Luke 18:20
Ten: You shall not covet	Exod. 20:17; Deut. 5:21	Luke 12:15–34

Life with Others (20:12–17)

The next six commandments have to do with human relationships. Being rightly related to God compels us toward right relationships with our neighbors. Within the covenant community, duties to God and duties to other human beings were not separated.

Honor parents (20:12). The ancient family was close-knit. Family loyalty was strong; family honor and respect were high. The purposes of the Israelite family included more than reproduction, instruction, and care giving. Families were also for the maintaining of traditions and conveying of wisdom. The fifth commandment emphasized the importance of parents in the community.

Do not murder (20:13). Great value is placed on human life; it is a sacred trust from God. The sixth commandment prohibited the unlawful killing of one human being by another as murder. To deliberately take the life of a human being usurps authority that belongs only to God. Since life is something which only God can give and sustain, no one has a right to choose to end a person's life.

Do not commit adultery (20:14). The seventh commandment shows that faithfulness to the marriage relationship is central in the divine will for human relationships. A marriage partner engaging in sexual intercourse with someone besides the other marriage partner is acting unfaithfully to the marriage relationship.

Do not steal (20:15). The eighth commandment prohibited taking another person's property without the person's consent. The more specific laws regarding stealing emphasized restoration of the stolen property to its lawful owner (22:1,4,7,9).

Do not give false testimony (20:16). Living in a covenant community would require the Israelites to take some responsibility for their neighbors within the community. They must respect the rights of a neighbor. The ninth commandment gave each neighbor a right to the truth. Testimony concerning a neighbor must be based on fact.

Do not covet (20:17). The tenth commandment prohibited any inordinate desire to possess what belongs to another. Coveting is sinful because it focuses greedily on the property of a neighbor. Such ungoverned and selfish desire threatens the basic rights of others.

- *A life guided by the Ten Commandments will*
- *reflect the nature of God Himself. When that*
- *reflection of God falls on our neighbors, the*
- *result will be justice, truth, and a righteous*
- *respect for the rights of others.*

BEFORE GOD AT MOUNT SINAI (20:18–21)

In the people's audience with God at Mount Sinai, the covenant bonding them and God in a special treaty had become a reality. The people expressed their need for a human mediator between them and the holy God. They feared that they might die from direct contact with such awesome power.

As mediator and spokesman for God, Moses would stand between the people and God, establishing the agreement or relationship between the two parties. He would receive the commandments on which the covenant was based and communicate them to the people. The task of guarding the relationship would also be his, and he would beseech God's mercy when the commandments and covenant were broken (Deut. 9:25–26).

■ As Israel's mediator, Moses represented God
■ to His people and His people to God. Today,
■ Christ alone is our mediator with God
■ (1 Tim. 2:5), guaranteeing full communion
■ with God for those placing faith in Him.

QUESTIONS TO GUIDE YOUR STUDY

1. Why does God demand complete loyalty from us? What are the "other gods" of our lives that compete for our attention?

2. How will living by the Ten Commandments help us to live together responsibly?

3. In what ways can we carry out the command to "honor" our parents?

The Lawgiver

The New Testament often identifies Moses as the intermediary through whom the Law was given: Jesus reminded the Jews, "Has not Moses given you the law? (John 7:19); and Paul referred to Moses when describing the institution of the Law, which "was put into effect through angels by a mediator" (Gal. 3:19).

The year spent at Mount Sinai in the southern Sinai peninsula was certainly a high point in Moses' life. Of all the events of that year, Moses no doubt was most affected by the time spent communing with God. Within the cloud on the top of the mountain, Moses received from God the Ten Commandments and the rest of the Law which he would deliver to Israel.

Most ancient treaties followed the general stipulations with a long list of specific demands or agreements. The specific stipulations of the Sinai covenant are known as the Book of the Covenant.

THE BOOK OF THE COVENANT (20:22–23:33)

During the making of the covenant between God and Israel on Mount Sinai, Moses read from "the Book of the Covenant" (24:7), and the people promised to obey. The contents of this "Book" included at least the material now found in Exod. 20:23–23:33.

The Nature of Proper Worship (20:22–26)

The stipulation of the code of laws begins at Exod. 21:1. First, however, God instructed Moses on how the people were to worship. To worship the Lord properly means establishing the proper place for worship as well as following a particular ritual of worship.

The Rights of Servants (21:1–11)

Slavery was a common practice among ancient Near Eastern peoples. Israel's laws concerned the humane treatment of servants and slaves, as well as their emancipation. As in other Near Eastern countries, Israel's slaves were considered property; yet as persons they also had rights.

Injuring or Killing Another Person (21:12–32)

Certain acts of wrongdoing were taken very seriously. Premeditated murder, attacking or cursing parents, and kidnapping another person were punishable by death. Wrongful deeds that caused personal loss or injury to another were settled by fines on the offender and compensation for the injured party.

■ *God made His people aware that they were*
■ *responsible to one another. They were to*
■ *treat everyone within the community with*
■ *justice. "Everyone" included parents, chil-*
■ *dren, servants, and neighbors.*

QUESTIONS TO GUIDE YOUR STUDY

1. How does the way in which the Hebrews treated their own servants differ from the treatment they themselves received as slaves in Egypt?
2. How does the principle of "eye for eye" limit the degree of retaliation in a punishment?

EXODUS 22

All things ultimately belong to God, and what He allows His people to possess becomes rightfully theirs to use. Israel was to respect another person's right to "own" property on loan from God.

Restitution

The principle of making restitution was based on a concept of equity. The stolen property was to be returned, or "full" compensation was to be made. In a case of lost or stolen property, some law codes prescribed a degree of retaliation against the guilty party, but Israel's law prescribed an equal payment to be made to the victim. In all community relationships, Israelites were to repay their obligations in full.

The Rights of the Property Owner (21:33–22:15)

The Israelites had been Egypt's slaves. Now they were free, traveling toward the Promised Land, and the ownership of property would become extremely important to them, even being regarded as a basic right. The law code established payments to be made to owners in various cases concerning the loss of personal property. The amount of repayment was determined by whether the person responsible for the loss was fully aware of his actions or whether he had planned these actions.

- *The principle of these laws was restitution.*
- *When we have taken something wrongfully*
- *or caused something to be lost or damaged,*
- *we must return or restore to the owner an*
- *equivalent payment. In this way, we live*
- *justly within God's covenant community.*

Returning the Cloak

In the dress customs of the Old Testament, the cloak served as an outer garment, which was also used as a night covering. Because of its daily use, the cloak was not an article of clothing to be loaned out. The covenant laws protected poor persons who were forced to relinquish their cloaks as pledge on a debt. Those holding the pledge must allow the debtor to sleep in the garment each night (22:26–27).

Responsibilities to Society (22:16–31)

Various laws aim at maintaining a moral society. Individuals were to conduct themselves responsibly toward each other and toward God. The worship of God was not to be corrupted by sorcery, sexual intercourse with animals, or other gods—common practices in the religions of other nations. Vulnerable members of society, such as virgins, aliens, widows, orphans, or debtors, were to be treated justly and with mercy. Responsible persons respected their ruler and gave their offerings to God.

QUESTIONS TO GUIDE YOUR STUDY

1. Many situations of our world are not covered by these laws. How can we apply the principle of restitution to our personal lives?

2. When we do someone wrong, why should we do even more than what might be expected to make things right?

3. Who are the vulnerable, helpless, or underprivileged people in our society who need our care and concern?

EXODUS 23 · · · · · · · · · · · · · · · · · ·

The Book of the Covenant addressed how the people were to treat each other as well as how they were to "treat" God. If they valued other people, they would respond to them with justice and mercy. If they valued God, they would respond with the proper rituals of worship.

Laws of Justice (23:1–9)

Injustice against anyone—rich or poor—is wrong. Israel's court system was to protect everyone, even the alien.

Sacred Occasions (23:10–19)

God's great acts of salvation in the lives of His people were remembered in regular religious celebrations. The annual festivals, called "festivals to the LORD" (Lev. 23:41), required the appearance of all males at the sanctuary. The Sabbath, the seventh day, was not only a day of rest following six work days but also a time to remember God's deliverance from Egypt (Deut. 5:15). The sabbath year, every seventh year, not only assured the continued fertility of the land by allowing it to lie fallow, but also protected the poor, who were allowed to eat from the natural abundance of the untended fields.

God Provides Guidance (23:20–33)

The Book of the Covenant closes with God's promise of protection. God ensures the well-being and survival of His people through His angel.

The angel of God symbolizes God's presence in an event, and this angel is identified with God Himself since God's name (that is, His nature and identity) was in the angel (23:21).

■ *The Book of the Covenant made clear the*
■ *specific stipulations of Israel's treaty with*
■ *God. If the Israelites fulfilled their responsi-*
■ *bilities within the covenant relationship and*
■ *did not make covenants with other gods, the*
■ *Lord would protect them and bring them vic-*
■ *tory. Victory would not come in a single*
■ *year; it would come on God's schedule.*

QUESTIONS TO GUIDE YOUR STUDY

1. What does it mean to worship God "properly" today? When, where, and how does proper worship take place?

2. Why should we be concerned about how we treat strangers, foreigners, and other outsiders?

3. Many people around us have different values than we do. Does treating people fairly mean we must adopt their differing values?

After all the laws and stipulations had been presented, God then confirmed the covenant in a mysterious ceremony.

SEALING AND PRESERVING THE COVENANT (24:1–18)

Contracting parties often sealed their agreement with oaths and a ceremony that included a fellowship meal. There were also procedures to be followed for storing the treaty. Now that God had finished conveying the laws to the people, the Sinai covenant must be sealed and preserved.

Ceremony of Sealing (24:1–11)

In a solemn ceremony involving a sacrifice as well as an oath sealed by blood and the covenant meal, God and His people ratified the Sinai covenant. The ceremony would represent outwardly the inward commitment of the people to do God's will as expressed in the covenant laws.

Some of the elders, as representatives of the people, were allowed to come nearer to the Lord, though not as near as Moses did. Among them were Nadab and Abihu, the older sons of Aaron. The privilege of participating so intimately in the ratification of the covenant should have left an imprint on them for the rest of their lives. Tragically, Aaron's sons would fail in their future role as Israel's priests (Lev. 10:1–5).

The people, who had earlier expressed their commitment to be a kingdom of priests for the Lord (19:6–8), now committed themselves to obey the covenant. The ceremony provided several visual reminders of their commitment.

Nadab and Abihu

Aaron's first and second sons, Nadab and Abihu, were participants in the covenant meal on Mount Sinai (24:9–11). For many people, an experience of such magnitude would have resulted in lifelong commitment to God. But later in their lives, Nadab and Abihu did what God had not commanded and were consumed by fire (Lev. 10:1–2). They failed to understand that their role was to lead others in the worship of God, not to experiment with new forms of "worship."

Stone pillars (24:4). Stone monuments or structures were set up as shrines to the gods, and Moses used twelve pillars, one for each of Israel's tribes.

Offerings and sacrifices (24:5). Israel was not unique among the nations of the ancient Near East in their use of sacrifices and offerings for religious expression. The sacrifices were the food and drink of the gods, and faithfulness in their presentation was an act of devotion.

Blood (24:6, 8). Blood was closely associated with human life. Its use in religious ceremony emphasized the sacredness of life.

Reading the covenant (24:7). Treaties often prescribed a regular public reading of the covenant. As the covenant law was read from the Book of the Covenant, the people could reflect upon and accept their responsibilities within the covenant relationship.

The covenant meal (24:11). The communal meal of the treaty partners served as a seal of the covenant. After the meal, Israel would begin living the covenant on a daily basis.

■ *In a public ceremony we confirm our com-*
■ *mitment to God's commands. The emotional*
■ *context of the ceremony should strengthen*
■ *our desire to carry out that commitment per-*
■ *sonally in our day-to-day lives.*

Preserving the Covenant (24:12–18)

The covenant or treaty texts also had to be prepared in duplicate and preserved in a safe place for regular, periodic reading. Moses therefore ascended the mountain to receive the tablets of stone which would be stored in the ark of the covenant (25:16). The only person accompanying Moses on this important trip up the mountain was Joshua, who himself was increasing in his leadership role in Israel (32:15–17).

■ *Producing a written form of a covenant and*
■ *storing that form was necessary for a legal*
■ *agreement; the written covenant would settle*
■ *any future controversy. Similarly, the Bible*
■ *serves as a written form of our present cove-*
■ *nant with God.*

QUESTIONS TO GUIDE YOUR STUDY

1. In what ceremonies of today's church do we commit ourselves publicly to obey God?
2. Once God's commandments are written and stored, why is "instruction" necessary?

EXODUS 25

The fourth section of the Book of Exodus, 25:1–31:18, focuses on the awe-inspiring presence of God. The Lord, who was worthy of worship, provided detailed rules for a worship place and for the priests who would minister there.

THE TABERNACLE AND PRIESTS

Once God and Israel had concluded the covenant, arrangements had to be made for God to live and reign among His people. These arrangements consisted of elaborate instructions for the building of a tabernacle—a tent where God would be worshiped (25:1–27:21). More

A Priest's Duties

The priests were in charge of sacrifice and offering at the worship place. While sacrificing was the priests' primary responsibility, other functions included blessing the people (Num. 6:22–26) and instructing them in the law of God (Deut. 31:9–12). One function, in particular, was reserved exclusively for the priest. Using the Urim and Thummim, the priests determined the will of God concerning matters affecting the community.

instructions outlined the furnishings for the tabernacle (30:1–31:18). In addition, God instructed Moses concerning the clothing and consecration of the priests, who would serve as personnel for the worship tent (28:1–29:46).

Offerings for the Tabernacle (25:1–9)

As their hearts moved them, the people were to give of their offerings for God's worship place. This tabernacle symbolized God's presence among His people, as God promised: "I will dwell among them" (25:8).

The Ark (25:10–22)

The original purpose of the ark was to be a container for the stone tablets upon which the Ten Commandments were inscribed. A slab of pure gold sat atop the ark. Often called the "mercy seat," it was the base for the golden cherubim, symbolizing the throne from which God ruled Israel (25:22).

Bread of the Presence

A table in the tabernacle held twelve sacred loaves of bread, which was set before the Lord as a continual offering (25:30). As new loaves were put out each Sabbath, the old bread was eaten by the priests (Lev. 24:5–9).

The Table (25:23–30)

On the table was placed the bread of the Presence, which represented God's presence and providential care.

The Lampstand (25:31–40)

The golden lampstand of the tabernacle was made with three branches extending from either side of a central tier. This candelabra, known as the menorah, later became symbolic of the nation Israel.

■ *The ark was the most important object*
■ *within the tabernacle, and inside the ark was*
■ *the Testimony, a copy of the Ten Command-*
■ *ments. Although the various pieces of sacred*

- *furniture were impressive, at their center*
- *would be the covenant agreement binding*
- *God and Israel.*

QUESTIONS TO GUIDE YOUR STUDY

1. Why does the atonement cover of the ark symbolize the throne of God?
2. How does each of these furniture pieces—the ark, the table, the lampstand—represent God as a *living* God?

EXODUS 26 ·

The tabernacle would also be known as the Tent of Meeting (Exod. 40:1), for this is where God would meet with His people.

INSTRUCTIONS FOR THE SANCTUARY

As a traveling people, the Israelites used tents for their personal dwelling places. The tabernacle was a sacred tent, a portable sanctuary, where Israel's God revealed Himself to His people and dwelled among them.

The Tabernacle (26:1–37)

Once built, the tabernacle would stand at the center of the camp (Num. 2:1–2). The directions given for its construction called for rich decorations and curtains. Curtains of goat hair and leather coverings of animal skins formed protective layers over the luxurious embroidered linen curtains of the interior. The structure was supported by wooden frames.

The Most Holy Place (vv. 31–37). The tabernacle was divided into two rooms by a curtain. The innermost room, called the Most Holy Place, formed one third of the tent and contained the ark with its atonement cover. In the outer two

71

Throughout Israel's history, a curtain separated the Most Holy Place from the Holy Place (26:33). Only the high priest could enter through that curtain, and he only once a year on the Day of Atonement. But at the time of Jesus' death, the curtain, then hanging in the Temple, was torn from top to bottom (Matt. 27:51). By His death, Jesus gained access to God for all who would come to God through Him.

thirds of the tent, called the Holy Place, was placed the lampstand and the table with the bread of the Presence.

■ *As impressive as the tabernacle would be, it*
■ *was only to be temporary. The significance*
■ *of this earthly tabernacle would be eclipsed*
■ *by the ministry of Christ (Heb. 9:11).*

QUESTIONS TO GUIDE YOUR STUDY

1. What furniture was put into the Holy Place?
2. What one item was located behind the curtain in the Most Holy Place?

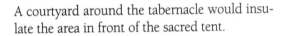

EXODUS 27

Horns of the Altar

The altar of burnt offering had four horns, one on each of its four corners (27:2). These horns were the place where blood from a sacrificial animal was applied for atonement from sin. In a graphic description of sin, the prophet Jeremiah spoke of sins so severe that they were engraved on the horns of the altar (Jer. 17:1).

A courtyard around the tabernacle would insulate the area in front of the sacred tent.

OUTSIDE THE TABERNACLE

The courtyard around the tabernacle isolated the sacred tent from the rest of the camp. Like the tabernacle itself, the courtyard was considered a holy place.

The Altar of Burnt Offering (27:1–8)

Somewhere before the door of the tabernacle was the altar of burnt offering, made of acacia wood overlaid with bronze. Upon this altar the sacrificial animals would be slaughtered. Blood from the sacrificed animals was applied to the horns of the altar for atonement from sin.

The Courtyard (27:9–19)

The court around the tabernacle was formed by curtains attached to poles. In the area of the courtyard before the tent was placed the altar of burnt offering and the laver.

Oil for the Lamps (27:20–21)

Oil was used as fuel for lamps, and olive oil would be plentiful in the land to which the Israelites were headed (Deut. 8:8). Light from the lampstand depicted God's divine presence.

■ *The courtyard was an area where prepara-*
■ *tions for worship took place. Our worship of*
■ *the Lord should not be haphazard, but*
■ *undertaken with forethought and detailed*
■ *preparation.*

QUESTIONS TO GUIDE YOUR STUDY

1. For what was olive oil used? What might have been the significance of continuous light throughout the night?
2. Who were responsible for maintaining the lampstand?

EXODUS 28

Aaron and his sons were the first officially appointed priests to serve at the tabernacle.

THE MEDIATOR OF GOD'S PRESENCE

The priests were mediators between God and the people. In this role, they were placed in charge of sacrifices and offerings at the tabernacle, God's worship place.

Holy Garments (28:1–5)

On Mount Sinai, God told Moses to appoint Aaron and his four sons to serve as priests—to serve at the altar and in the sanctuary. The garments that they were to wear would symbolize the prestige of their priestly role. Outer garments included an ephod with waistband, a breastpiece, and a robe. Underneath these items, the priest wore a linen undergarment and a tunic with a sash. The ensemble was completed by the turban.

The Ephod (28:6–14)

From descriptions in the Old Testament the ephod appears to have been a simple, linen garment, possibly a short skirt, apron, or loincloth. It was worn over the priest's robe, but under his breastpiece. The ephod was fastened around the waist by a beautiful and intricately woven waistband (28:8), to which the breastpiece was attached.

The Breastpiece (28:15–30)

As the high priest ministered in the tabernacle, he wore upon his breast a piece of elaborate embroidery about nine inches square, which was securely tied to the ephod. This breastpiece, or breastplate, was set with twelve stones, each stone engraved with the name of one of the twelve tribes of Israel. Inside the breastpiece were placed two stones, the Urim and Thummim. Since these stones were the means of making decisions of judgment, the garment itself was called the "breastpiece of decision" (28:29–30).

The Priest's Clothes (28:31–43)

Various other items completed the priest's attire. Equally elaborate as the ephod was the robe worn with it. The distinctive headdress or turban dis-

Urim and Thummim

Little is known about the Urim and Thummim. They were objects used by the high priest to determine God's will, probably serving as sacred lots. An example of how they were used appears in 1 Sam. 14:41–45. To receive an answer to a question, the high priest perhaps drew or shook the Urim and Thummim from a bag. One object gave one answer; the other, another answer. The lot which came out first may have been accepted as God's answer.

played a golden plate with the engraving, "holy to the LORD" (28:36). A loose-fitting tunic made of linen hung from the neck to probably the ankles, being tied with a sash, while a linen undergarment extended from waist to thigh.

■ *The unique garments of the high priest estab-*
■ *lished his identity as a mediator between the*
■ *people and their God. The garments were*
■ *considered sacred, and the priest must wash*
■ *before dressing (Lev. 16:4). Entering God's*
■ *presence was a privilege not to be taken*
■ *lightly. By wearing the special clothing, the*
■ *priest would signal his proper attitude*
■ *toward God and sacred matters.*

QUESTIONS TO GUIDE YOUR STUDY

1. Which items of the high priest's attire symbolized his function as the people's representative before God?
2. What meaning is expressed by our religious dress of today?
3. How do we show respect for religious leaders in our churches today?

EXODUS 29

An elaborate ceremony would symbolize the people's acceptance of Aaron and his sons as their spiritual leaders and representatives before God.

CONSECRATION OF THE PRIESTS (29:1–46)

When priests were consecrated, they were separated to God. They were considered to be holy

Consecrate

Consecration refers to persons or things being separated to or belonging to God. Other English words convey a sense similar to *consecrate,* such as "make holy," "hallow," "sanctify," and "dedicate." During the ritual of consecration, parts of the sacrifice were placed in the hands of the priests, possibly as a symbol of the priests' sacrificing responsibility (29:22–24).

and to belong to God. They were set apart to live according to God's demands and in His service.

As with most ancient Near Eastern peoples, the consecration of priests entailed a great amount of ritual. Sacrifices were used in the ordination ritual; a bull was slaughtered as a sin offering. Other sacrifices provided Aaron and his sons a holy meal. These sacrifices were repeated each day for a week as a part of the ordination ceremony.

Another part of the ceremony involved dressing the priests in the sacred garments. The ritual was made even more elaborate with baths and anointing with oil and with blood. The purpose of such ritual was to ensure that a priest who would serve God would be clean and pure. Only then was the priest prepared to enter God's presence and represent the people before Him.

■ *God wanted all His people to share His pres-*
■ *ence, but they could not treat the divine pres-*
■ *ence casually. The place where they would*
■ *meet God was to be considered holy. Special*
■ *rites for the priests not only purified them for*
■ *service but also impressed upon all observers*
■ *the holiness of God.*

QUESTIONS TO GUIDE YOUR STUDY

1. The Israelites were to be a "kingdom of priests," so why was it necessary for God to establish the position of high priest?

2. What procedures in the ritual of consecration emphasized God's holiness?

Various items were needed to sustain continuous worship at the tabernacle. The burning of incense would symbolize the constant prayers of the people. The annual atonement money would be a continuous ransom for the people's lives. The washing basin would purify the priests before each time of service.

The Altar of Incense (30:1–10)

Like the altar of burnt offering, the altar of incense had horns on the four corners. It was constructed of acacia wood, overlaid with gold. As the altar's name implied, incense was burned on this altar, serving as a sweet smelling offering that would be pleasing to God. The altar was placed in the Holy Place, along with the table and lampstand.

The Census Offering (30:11–16)

Moses was instructed to take a census of the Israelites. This enumeration of the population might have been needed to determine the availability of manpower for a war (Num. 1:2–3). Another purpose was for taxation: a half-shekel tax was assessed on each male over twenty. The people were to give this tax, called "atonement money," as an offering to the Lord for the support of the tabernacle.

The Washing Basin (30:17–21)

A large basin or bowl, often called a laver, was used in purification rites. Located in the courtyard, between the tabernacle and the altar of burnt offering, it was used by the priests to wash their hands and feet before they performed their priestly service.

Altar of Incense

The altar of incense was smaller than the altar of burnt offering. Only the high priest burned incense on this altar, and he was to use only the precise blend of spices in the incense. Once a year, on the Day of Atonement, the priest sprinkled blood on the horns of the altar (Lev. 16:18–19).

In the ancient Near East, domestic oil was prepared from olives. Archaeologists have found around Palestine abundant evidence of stone presses, used for extracting oil from olives. This oil, called "beaten oil," was lighter and considered the best oil. After the beaten oil was extracted, another grade of oil was produced by heating the pulp and pressing it again.

Oil for Anointing (30:22–33)

Oil was used extensively for religious ceremonies in biblical times. The ritual of anointing involved rubbing or smearing a person or object with oil to set them apart for God's service. Priests were ceremonially anointed in this manner as a sign of official appointment to office; the anointing symbolized God's power upon them. The ritual was carried out with an element of awe.

Holy Incense (30:34–38)

A mixture of aromatic spices was prepared to be burned in connection with the offering of sacrifices (Exod. 25:6). Because this incense was for use in worship, it was considered holy and had to be prepared according to exacting specifications.

■   *The bad effects of human sin can be*
■   *removed only through atonement. To*
■   *restore fellowship with God, the peo-*
■ *ple were to make an offering of blood from a*
■ *sacrificed animal or of ransom money. Our*
■ *atonement today is focused on the cross of*
■ *Christ. He paid our ransom money (Mark*
■ *10:45); He gave His blood to redeem us*
■ *(1 Pet. 1:18–19).*

QUESTIONS TO GUIDE YOUR STUDY

1. How often did Aaron sprinkle blood on the altar of incense?
2. In what way did the atonement money differ from the offerings that were received for the tabernacle (Exod. 25:1)?
3. The Israelites used incense and oil for several purposes. Why did the incense and oil for the tabernacle have to be different?

The Lord's last instructions to Moses on the mountain were for the construction of the tabernacle. The work would be supervised by skilled craftsmen whom God had already chosen. While building a worship place was an important task, the people must involve themselves with this project only on six days of the week. The Sabbath was to remain holy.

SKILLED CRAFTSMEN (31:1–11)

Craftsmen would respond to God's presence by dedicating their God-given skills to the building of the tabernacle and its furnishings. Bezalel, from the tribe of Judah, was a great grandson of Caleb (1 Chron. 2:18–20). His skill derived from his being filled with the Spirit of God. Oholiab, from the tribe of Dan, was the craftsman and designer who assisted Bezalel in the tabernacle's construction.

Bezalel and Oholiab had mastered an occupation requiring manual dexterity and artistic skill. They were not only woodworkers and carpenters, but also metalworkers, skilled, learned in working with gold, silver, and bronze. Further, they were stonecutters, able to dress and set cut stones.

 As God's people, we are responsible to use whatever gifts He has given us to accomplish His purposes.

The Sabbath (31:12–17)

The seventh day, the Sabbath, was a token of the covenant relation between God and His people. So important was the observance of the Sabbath that the penalty for desecration of this day was death (31:14). For six days the Israelites could work, but on the seventh they must rest. This requirement also applied to all slaves, foreigners, and beasts. One reason to observe the Sabbath was because God rested on the seventh day after creation, thereby making the day holy (Exod. 20:11).

■ *When we observe the Lord's Day—the*
■ *Christian's Sabbath day—we honor and rec-*
■ *ognize God as the Lord of creation, who in*
■ *six days created the heavens and the earth,*
■ *and rested on the seventh day.*

The Stone Tablets (v. 18).

These tablets were perhaps small steles such as those other nations used to publicize their laws. What made these tablets unique was that they had been inscribed by "the finger of God." In this picturesque expression of God at work, the finger of God writing the Ten Commandments illustrated God's giving the Law without any mediation (Deut. 9:10).

Tablets of Stone

Various names are given for the stone objects on which the Ten Commandments were written. They are called the "tablets of stone," the "tablets of the covenant" (Deut. 9:9), and the "tablets of the Testimony" (Exod. 31:18). These tablets provided a flat surface for writing. They were perhaps small steles such as those used by other nations to publicize their laws.

■ *Recording something in writing gives a per-*
■ *manence to the spoken word. Nothing could*
■ *be more permanent or more unchangeable*
■ *than that which is written in stone by the fin-*
■ *ger of God.*

QUESTIONS TO GUIDE YOUR STUDY

1. Why is it important to remember that our talents and abilities are really gifts from God?

2. What was the purpose of establishing the seventh day as the Sabbath?

3. Other nations in Israel's time had written law codes of their own. What made Israel's tablets of stone unique?

EXODUS 32 · · · · · · · · · · · · · · · · · ·

The fifth section of the Book of Exodus, 32:1–34:35, focuses on the disciplining and forgiving presence of God. Even though a disobedient people broke the covenant, a forgiving God initiated restoration—but not without administering punishment.

BREAKING THE COVENANT (32:1–35)

Israel refused to take their covenant commitment seriously almost from the start. While Moses remained on the mountain in God's presence to receive the Ten Commandments, the people were already breaking one of those commandments. Their impatience led to disobedience.

The Golden Calf (32:1–6)

The covenant fellowship between the Lord and the Israelites almost immediately fell on hard times. Even before Moses could descend from the mountain with the tables of stone and other covenant texts, the people violated the covenant terms. As Moses delayed on the mountain, the people asked Aaron for action, crying "Make us gods" (32:1).

Aaron obliged, making a calf and apparently leading in its worship. The people's sin obviously involved rejecting the second commandment: "You shall not make for yourself an idol" (20:4). Yet since they were worshiping a calf in addition to the Lord (32:4–5), they also broke

The Golden Calf

The image that Aaron made for the people was probably an image of a young bull, constructed of wood and overlaid with gold. Living bulls were important in the religion of some regions of ancient Egypt. Bull images also appear in the art and religious texts of Mesopotamia, Asia Minor, Phoenicia, and Syria. Aaron's image was apparently intended to represent the Lord (32:5), but such action was still in violation of the second commandment (20:4–6).

the first commandment: "You shall have no other gods" (20:3).

■ *It is easy for people to form and shape for*
■ *themselves gods with which they are com-*
■ *fortable and familiar—gods that agree with*
■ *them. Tragically, our relationship with the*
■ *sovereign Lord is damaged by any substitute*
■ *god we allow into our hearts.*

God's Wrath Against a Disobedient People (32:7–14)

The people's act of apostasy brought God's judgment and even a threat of annihilation. Yet God's comment to Moses, "Now leave me alone" (32:10), was possibly a test of Moses. Would Moses step aside and watch an angry God destroy a sinful people? Or would Moses assume his role as a mediator between the people and God?

Moses prayed for God's mercy, calling on God to remember His reputation among the nations as well as His promises to the patriarchs. As a result, God relented. Through intercessory prayer, Moses sought to make an atonement for sin, identifying himself so completely with the people that he asked to be blotted out of God's book if God would not forgive the people's sin (32:30–32). Moses was a true mediator.

Abraham's Covenant

Moses reminded God about His covenant with Abraham (32:13). That covenant involved divine promises; God promised to give the land of Canaan to Abraham's descendants after a long sojourn to a foreign land. The promises extended to include international relations, many descendants, and to be God of Abraham's descendants forever (Gen. 17:3–8). Moses knew that he and the multitude of people he was leading were heirs to those covenant promises.

■ *God could destroy the people and be a true*
■ *God of justice. He could forgive the people*
■ *and be a true God of mercy. Either action*
■ *would have been consistent with God's*

■ nature. *Moses' intercessory plea for God to*
■ *honor His covenant with the patriarchs made*
■ *the difference.*

The Lord Relented

Judgment on a Disobedient People (32:15–29)

Before an angry God, Moses had prayed for the people in spite of their sin. But when he came down from the mountain and actually saw the people's sin, he reacted angrily and threw the tablets with the Law to the ground, breaking them. The broken tablets visually represented what had taken place with the people. The tablets and their writing were the "work of God" (32:16), but so were the laws and commandments spoken by God which established the covenant relationship. A broken commandment had produced a broken relationship, a broken covenant, and now the broken tablets.

Aaron was unwilling to accept the responsibility he bore. He blamed the people first for having an evil tendency (32:22) and then for lacking trust in Moses (32:23). Finally he tried to suggest that the calf magically appeared (32:24). But he could not, or would not, face the truth: as the people's leader in Moses' absence, he had failed to represent the Lord.

Moses put a stop to the idolatry by forcing the people to make a choice—either for the Lord or for the golden calf, but not for both. The tribe of Levi was the only tribe that chose to stand with Moses against the people who were worshiping the calf. For their actions, God chose the Levites to be priests for Israel.

The Hebrew word translated "to relent" can also be translated "to repent." To repent means to reorient oneself from sin to God. In this sense, of course, God does not repent like humans. But repentance can mean merely a feeling of regret or a changing of the mind. In this sense, God does repent or relent. God regretted He had created the human race (Gen. 6:6), and He changed His mind about destroying His disobedient people (Exod. 32:14).

■ *One man, Moses, was so emotionally bur-*
■ *dened by the people's sin that he burned with*

Atonement

Atonement, meaning "reconciliation," was associated with sacrificial offerings to remove the effects of sin. In the Old Testament, atonement refers to the process God established whereby humans could make an offering to God to restore fellowship with God. Theologians have understood atonement both as *expiation,* meaning to remove the barrier that sin creates, as well as *propitiation,* meaning to appease an angry God. Following the people's sin with the golden calf, Moses, as their mediator, sought to make atonement for them (32:30).

■ righteous anger. Another man, Aaron, was
■ so intent on escaping personal responsibility
■ that he felt no remorse for his own sin.

Punishment of a Disobedient People (32:30–35)

The Lord was attentive to Moses' cry and did not utterly destroy the idolaters immediately. Nevertheless, the mediator's majestic intercession was not sufficient to allow the people to escape the consequences of their sin. The plague by which they were punished (32:35) is not identified elsewhere in the Bible.

■ If God had dismissed the people's sin, allow-
■ ing them to bear no responsibility for their
■ disobedience, He would have violated His
■ nature as a God of righteousness.

QUESTIONS TO GUIDE YOUR STUDY

1. Why do people create false gods to worship?

2. What important role did Aaron play in producing the golden idol? How many different scenarios did he offer to hide his role?

3. Was Moses' violent reaction against the people's false worship justified?

EXODUS 33 · · · · · · · · · · · · · · · · · ·

Moses was willing to give up his place in God's book in exchange for the people's forgiveness. Only a leader who communed with God face to face could develop such an attitude.

RESTORING THE COVENANT
RELATIONSHIP (33:1–23)

The people were punished, but God relented of His threat to destroy them. The question now concerned the future of the covenant relationship between God and His people: Could it be completely restored or was it irreparably torn?

A Disobedient People Repent (33:1–6)

There were difficult lessons to learn about maintaining a relationship with a holy God. One lesson was that God would withdraw His immediate presence from a sinful people (33:3). The Lord declared that He could not go with Israel lest He destroy the stubborn, rebellious people.

God did renew His promise to bring His people into the new land, even promising an angel to ensure their well being and survival. Yet this angel was a substitute for the personal presence of God, a substitution that led the Israelites to sincere repentance. By taking off their ornaments (33:6), they showed a new willingness to obey.

- A holy God cannot dwell in the midst of an
- unholy people. God's mercy and the people's
- repentance made it possible for the two sides
- to come together again.

The Tent of Meeting (33:7–11)

God showed His continued presence in the Tent of Meeting, but this location "outside the camp" (33:7) actually symbolized distance between God and the people because of their sin. God's intimacy with Moses highlighted the Holy One's separation from Israel even more. Apparently,

Tents of Meeting

The Book of Exodus mentions two tents, both of which are considered a tent "of meeting" where God met with the people. First, after the sin with the golden calf, a provisional tabernacle was established outside the camp and called the "tent of meeting" (33:7). Second, a more permanent tabernacle was built in accordance with directions given to Moses by God on Mount Sinai. This tent was called both the "Tent of the Testimony" (Num. 17:7) and the "Tent of Meeting" (Exod. 29:42).

only Moses actually entered the tent to meet God, disappearing behind a pillar of cloud while the people watched. The young Joshua protected and cared for the tent. As Moses' servant, Joshua was replacing Aaron, who had discredited himself with the golden calf.

 Very few humans would dare speak to God the way they speak to earthly friends, but Moses did. Significantly, Jesus has opened the way for us to be "friends" with the divine (John 15:15).

The Glory of the Lord (33:12–23)

In another intimate moment with God, Moses sought assurance of God's presence. Having received the promise of divine presence for the journey ahead, Moses desired even more. In response to Moses' request for a unique, visible manifestation, God allowed His glory to pass by Moses. But this revelation did not reveal all of God, for no person can see the entirety of the divine glory, not even Moses (33:20).

■ *God chooses not to reveal Himself in spectac-*
■ *ular visible manifestations. He will not put*
■ *on a heavenly fireworks show. But He will*
■ *reveal Himself in mercy and compassion.*

QUESTIONS TO GUIDE YOUR STUDY

1. What does it mean to be spiritually "stiff-necked"?
2. What was Moses' offer to God as he pleaded for God to be present with the people?

Presence

The "presence" of God is God's own initiative in encountering people. God is free to be where God wills, but He chooses to be with His people to give them life.

Israel experienced God's presence in various ways. The presence was related to the tabernacle, the place for Israel to encounter God in worship. Perhaps the primary tangible symbol of God's presence with the people was the ark of the covenant—the container for the tablet of the laws—and the seat of God's throne. The cloud and fire symbolized the presence leading on the journey to Canaan.

3. Why did Moses find such great favor with God?

EXODUS 34 · · · · · · · · · · · · · · · ·

Moses had asked God for a guarantee of His presence, not only to be with him but with the people as well. Israel had experienced a disciplining God; now they would experience a forgiving God.

RENEWING THE COVENANT (34:1–35)

The covenant at Mount Sinai was initiated by God, and now only God could restore the covenant relationship. God's mercy and compassion—not Israel's faithfulness—formed the basis for renewal of the broken covenant.

A New Set of Tablets (34:1–9)

The first step was to prepare a second set of stone tablets to replace the broken set. On this occasion, the Lord revealed Himself to Moses as a God of mercy and compassion (34:6–7). Again, Moses sought the assurance of God's presence (34:8–9).

God's Forgiving Presence (34:10–28)

God renewed the covenant with His people, making explicit His covenant promise to conquer miraculously the land of Canaan promised to Abraham. The renewed covenant, like the original one, involved Israel's pledge to make no other covenants (34:12, 15). Also involved were God's commandments as His expectations for the covenant people. Some of the commandments of Exod. 34:17–26 appeared in the first covenant (Exod. 20:22–23:19).

Three Festivals

At three annual festivals all males were required to appear at the sanctuary (34:23). These occasions were times when freewill offerings were made (Deut. 16:16–17). Passover and the Feast of Unleavened Bread were the first festival, occurring in the spring. The second was the Feast of Weeks (also called the Feast of Harvest), celebrated seven weeks later. The third was the Feast of Tabernacles (also called the Feast of Ingathering), celebrated in the fall at the closing of the grape harvest.

God revealed another aspect of His character by revealing another of His names: Jealous (34:14). The jealous God is intolerant of rivalry from other gods. The Lord will not share His people's allegiance with deities worshiped by other peoples. One way in which God's jealousy for Israel would show itself was in God's protection of His people from enemies.

- *God would be merciful to a disobedient peo-*
- *ple. God would be forgiving. Yet God would*
- *also be jealous. He will not allow us to divide*
- *our loyalties between Him and whatever life-*
- *style unbelievers offer us.*

The Radiance of God (34:29–35)

Descending from the mountain with the tablets of the covenant, Moses appeared before his people, his face aglow with the reflection of God's glory. Such intense communication with God over an extended period of time had brought radiance to Moses' face. After this time, Moses veiled his face, except when he spoke to God and delivered God's messages to the people.

- *Closeness with God changed Moses' appear-*
- *ance. Our close encounters with God may*
- *not be identical to what Moses experienced;*
- *nevertheless, time spent with God will*
- *change us—and change us for the better.*

QUESTIONS TO GUIDE YOUR STUDY

1. What two names for Himself did God mention to Moses in this meeting on Mount Sinai?
2. What did it mean for Israel to be God's inheritance?
3. What harm would come to Israel for making a treaty with some of the nations in the land to which they were journeying?

EXODUS 35

The sixth and final section of the Book of Exodus, 35:1–40:38, focuses on the abiding presence of God. God honored the obedience of His people with His holy presence.

AN OBEDIENT, WORSHIPING COMMUNITY (35:1–39:43)

Exodus concludes with Israel's response to God's offer of forgiveness. Without delay, the work of tabernacle construction got underway. The account of this building duplicates the Lord's instructions to Moses on the tabernacle in Exod. 25–31, but the setting is different. In the earlier chapters, God spoke to Moses concerning His plans for dwelling with His people. Now Moses spoke to the whole Israelite community concerning God's commands, giving them an opportunity to respond in obedience

Moses Tells of God's Commandments (35:1–3)

As Moses related the specific requirements to the people, he began with the stipulation concerning the Sabbath day. Every seventh day the people were to rest in recognition and worship

Paul and Moses' Veil

For the apostle Paul, Moses' veil illustrated the superiority of the new covenant. Israel saw the fading splendor of the era of death reflected in Moses' face, but Christians see the abiding splendor of the era of the Spirit and God-given righteousness (2 Cor. 3:7–11).

Moses' veil further illustrated the mental barrier which prevented Israel from recognizing Christ in the Old Testament (2 Cor. 3:12–15). Through faith in Christ the veil is removed, and believers enjoy free access to God which transforms life (2 Cor. 3:15–18).

Spinning Cloth

Skilled women worked on the tabernacle, spinning yarn and linen (35:25). Raw materials were spun and woven into fabric sections about six feet in width and as long as necessary. Egyptian murals indicate that the looms used by the women were large and technologically advanced.

of the God of creation and redemption. They must not involve themselves even in God's work, constructing the tabernacle, on that day.

Providing Resources for God's Work (35:4–19)

Although Moses related to the people "what the LORD has commanded" (35:4), their response was not coerced. Only those who were "willing" were to bring the offerings and materials needed for the tabernacle construction. Not only were the people to provide supplies but workmanship as well. Those who were "skilled" (35:10) were called to do the work of making everything according to plan.

- *Give not what you are requested to give but*
- *what you truly want to give. This principle of*
- *stewardship is a familiar one: The apostle*
- *Paul likewise urged his readers to give cheer-*
- *fully, not reluctantly (2 Cor. 9:7).*

Providing Resources and Skills (35:20–29)

Through Moses, God called His people to establish a place of worship. The response of the obedient people was thrilling and moving as they provided the skills and supplies needed for God's work. Both men and women (35:22, 29) gave willingly of their possessions and of themselves.

QUESTIONS TO GUIDE YOUR STUDY

1. What group of people did *not* contribute to the tabernacle project?
2. Why was it important for Moses, as he led the people into the tabernacle project, to begin with a reminder about observing the Sabbath?

EXODUS 36

The project began with the building of the tabernacle frames and the making of the curtains.

Artistic Craftsmanship (35:30–36:7)
Bezalel and Oholiab were the skilled craftsmen responsible for making the tabernacle, its furnishings, and trappings. They were not only skillful in their own craftsmanship; they were also able to "teach others" (35:34), so there was no shortage of workers. Nor was there a lack of materials; indeed, the people contributed more than enough (36:6, 7).

Building God's Dwelling Place (36:8–38)
Detail by detail, the people constructed the sacred tent according to God's plan. The community must have been buzzing with activity—some building, some sewing, some designing. Constructing an elaborate tent like the tabernacle was no small task in a wilderness environment.

- ■ *Those people who give for God's purposes*
- ■ *and do so willingly from a cheerful heart will*
- ■ *discover that their giving more than meets*
- ■ *the current needs.*

QUESTIONS TO GUIDE YOUR STUDY
1. What were the strengths and talents that Bezalel brought to the job?
2. What gifts has God's Spirit given you? How can you use your gifts effectively for God's purposes?
3. If we compare the account of the people's work (Exod. 36:8–38) with the account

Each of the six branches of the golden lampstand may have had a seven-spouted lamp. In Zechariah's vision of the gold lampstand, the prophet saw seven lights, each with seven channels (Zech. 4:2). Lamps often had a pinched spout to support the wick, which was generally made of twisted flax. The wicks generally burned olive oil.

of God's instructions (Exod. 26), do we find that they omitted some steps to make the job easier?

EXODUS 37

The constructing of the tabernacle is reported first, then the making of the furnishings. In actuality, work probably proceeded on many of these objects simultaneously.

Furnishings for the Interior (37:1–29)

The construction of the sacred furnishings for the tabernacle is reported in a particular order. The account first mentions the items to be placed inside the tent. The only item in the Most Holy Place was the ark. The Holy Place contained the table for the bread of the Presence, the lampstand, and the altar of incense.

EXODUS 38

The account in Exod. 37–38 provides much detail, describing how the people constructed the tabernacle and its furnishings. These chapters could have been reduced to this statement: "The Israelites did all the work just as the Lord commanded Moses."

The Courtyard and Its Furnishings (38:1–20)

In the courtyard in front of the tabernacle was the washing basin and the altar of burnt offering. The bronze basin was constructed from metal mirrors provided by the women who ministered at the tabernacle entrance (38:8). These women are mentioned only one other time in the Bible (1 Sam. 2:22). Such a lack of information makes it impossible to know who they were or what ministerial service they provided.

An Inventory of Materials (38:21–31)

Ithamar, Aaron's fourth son, was apparently in charge of the Levites; and he supervised an inventory of materials used in the tabernacle project. Even though the tabernacle was being built in the desert, the leaders made a careful accounting of all the offerings that had been entrusted to them. The inventory shows the generosity of the Israelites in contributing to the new worship place. Bezalel and Oholiab (38:22, 23) are credited with crafting everything according to God's instructions.

Weights were used in a balance to weigh out silver and gold, and the shekel was the basic unit of weight in the Hebrew system. One talent was equal to three thousand shekels. Hebrew weights, however, were never an exact system; and the talent and shekel of the tabernacle inventory may not have represented values that they had later in Israel's history.

An accounting was made of all the materials used to build the tabernacle. We should be as diligent about tracking the use of resources for God's work as we are in tracking our own personal resources.

QUESTIONS TO GUIDE YOUR STUDY

1. How many different names are used for the tabernacle?
2. Which of Israel's twelve tribes was responsible for taking the inventory of materials used in the tabernacle?

Israel was a nation of considerable size, requiring a formal worship with a formal priesthood. The holy garments for the priests were made precisely as prescribed; these garments were worn before the Lord and had to be complete in every detail.

Garments for the Priests (39:1–31)

Priestly dress consisted of only the best of fine linen, with gold threads interwoven into the fabric. The sacred garments—including the ephod, the breastpiece, the robe, tunics, turbans, headbands, undergarments, and sashes—were made exactly "as the LORD commanded Moses" (39:1). There is no mention of the Urim and Thummim (28:30) in chapter 39 since these sacred lots were probably natural stones.

The Tabernacle Work Completed (39:32–43)

Once finished with their work, the people brought everything to Moses for his inspection. Since they had done the work "just as the LORD had commanded," Moses gave them his blessing (39:42–43).

The Ephod

From the earliest uses of the ephod, this priestly garment appears to have been associated with the presence of God. When not being worn by the high priest, the ephod was apparently displayed in the tabernacle. The design was very ornate. On top of each of the shoulders, the ephod was fastened by an onyx clasp on which were engraved the names of six of the twelve tribes of Israel.

■ *The people had been faithful in bringing the*
■ *materials needed for construction. They had*
■ *been generous with their time, using their*
■ *skills and abilities to complete the work. Pre-*
■ *viously Moses had described them as a "stiff-*
■ *necked people," but now he could call them*
■ *an obedient people.*

QUESTIONS TO GUIDE YOUR STUDY

1. How did the craftsmen prepare the gold thread that was woven into the colored yarn?

2. What aspect of the tabernacle story suggests that God takes an interest in the small details of our personal lives?

3. As the leader, how did Moses carry out his responsibility to oversee the people's work?

The Blessing

The Old Testament world had a unique concept of the spoken word, especially in the context of worship or other formal settings, that is important for understanding the significance of a blessing. In these thought patterns, the formally spoken word had both an independent existence and the power of it own fulfillment. Formal words of blessing also had the same power of self-fulfillment. Blessing released suprahuman powers which could bring to pass the content of the blessing. Moses amply rewarded the Israelites for their work when he "blessed them" (39:43).

EXODUS 40

Moses' leadership role involved the establishment of a worship place and worship practices. He showed the people when, where, and how to worship. The last task was to set everything up.

PREPARING FOR WORSHIP (40:1–38)

The original "tent of meeting" (33:7) was a provisional edifice where God met with His people. This tent, however, did not become a national sanctuary. It contained neither an ark nor those items necessary for worship. No priests served at this "tent of meeting." It was time for the leader of God's people to set up the place where Israel would worship.

Erecting the Tabernacle (40:1–33)

Moses followed carefully the Lord's instructions for setting up the tabernacle and establishing worship in it. The task involved more than just erecting the structure and placing all the furnishings in the correct location. Each item had to be consecrated—anointed with oil—since it was holy and was being set apart for God's service (40:9).

Even the day for setting up the tabernacle was given: The first day of the first month (40:1). It was now the beginning of the "second year" (40:17) since Israel had left Egypt. Eleven and one-half months earlier, they had witnessed the final plague in Egypt (12:2,6). Now they were constructing a worship place for the God who had delivered them by that plague.

■ *Moses set the example for us to follow in our*
■ *Christian service. He finished the task; like-*
■ *wise, our jobs for God must not be left half*
■ *done. More importantly, Moses completed*
■ *his task "as the LORD commanded him." We*
■ *must give careful attention to every detail of*
■ *God's assignments.*

Entering the Presence

The large basin for washing was placed before the tabernacle. Moses and the priests were careful to wash before entering the sacred tent or ministering at the altar of incesne (40:32). Likewise, we should take extra care to prepare ourselves for entering the presence of God. Are we clean (inside)? Have we washed our hands (of deeds)? Have we observed the character and actions that allow God's people to share His presence?

God's Presence Fills the Worship Place (40:34–38)

At last "Moses finished the work" (40:33), all according to the explicit instruction of the Lord and through the wisdom of His Spirit. God blessed Moses' actions by filling the tabernacle with His holy, glorious presence.

Like the provisional tent (33:7), the tabernacle was also called the Tent of Meeting (40:6, 22, 34). A cloud had descended on the first tent whenever Moses came to inquire of God; but the cloud stayed on the permanent tabernacle, and the awesome glory of God filled it so even Moses himself could not enter it.

The tabernacle fulfilled some of God's promises to the people. There He would meet with them (29:43), and there He would "dwell among the Israelites and be their God" (29:45). By cloud and fire God revealed His presence among the people of Israel, whether the tabernacle was at rest or in transit. He would be with them each step of the journey to the sacred tent's final earthly destination in Canaan.

- *God revealed His great glory in such a*
- *majestic way that even Moses could not view*
- *it. Most of all, He revealed His will to be*
- *present among His people and to lead them*
- *through their daily activities.*

QUESTIONS TO GUIDE YOUR STUDY

1. What are some of the jobs in your church that still need to be finished? How would God want the job to be done?
2. How did God demonstrate to the Israelites His desire to dwell in their midst?
3. How did the Israelites, on a daily basis, show their complete trust in God?

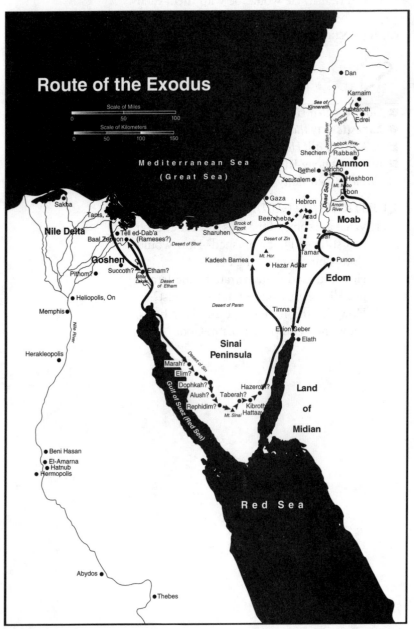

Adapted from *Holman Bible Handbook*, (Nashville, Tenn.: Broadman & Holman Publishers, 1992), p. 169.

The following is a collection of source works that will provide either more specific information on the book of Exodus or an expanded treatment of themes and topics related to Exodus.

Cate, Robert L. *Exodus.* (Layman's Bible Book Commentary, vol. 3). A popular-level treatment of the Book of Exodus. This easy-to-use volume provides a relevant and practical perspective for the reader.

Cate, Robert L. *An Introduction to the Old Testament and Its Study.* A popular introduction for the college and seminary level that introduces each individual Old Testament book and discusses its background, outline, significance, and relationship to the whole.

Holman Bible Dictionary. An exhaustive, alphabetically arranged resource of Bible-related subjects. An excellent tool of definitions and other information on the people, places, things, and events of the Book of Exodus.

Holman Bible Handbook. A comprehensive treatment of Exodus that offers outlines, commentary on key themes and sections, illustrations, charts, maps, and full-color photos. Provides an emphasis on the broader theological message of Exodus.

Disciple's Study Bible. A study Bible offering more than 10,000 annotations on the Bible. A valuable resource for relating the message of Exodus to the key doctrines of the Christian faith. Provides a theological introduction to each book of the Bible, as well as insights for putting faith into practice.

SHEPHERD'S NOTES

SHEPHERD'S NOTES